ADVERTISING
FOR SKEPTICS

Bob Hoffman

Advertising For Skeptics by Bob Hoffman

Cover Design: Jean Robaire
Interior Design: Bonnie Miguel
Publisher: Type A Group, LLC
For information contact: bob@typeagroup.com

ISBN 978-0-9992307-3-2

Also by Bob Hoffman

101 Contrarian Ideas About Advertising

Marketers Are From Mars, Consumers Are From New Jersey

BadMen

Laughing@Advertising

About Bob

"If you don't know who Bob Hoffman is then you really don't work in advertising. That, or you have not steeped yourself in the wisdom of this man." *MediaPost*

"One of our truly great marketing iconoclasts" *Prof. Mark Ritson*

"I'm jealous. I wish I was brave enough to be this rude." *Prof. Byron Sharp*

"The most provocative man in advertising." *Fuel Lines*

"Fabulously irreverent." *Time, Inc, UK*

"Bob Hoffman is a wicked acid-tongued genius!" *Ted Griggs, NBC*

"Bob Hoffman...is possibly going to be seen as the most influential person of the decade when it comes to media." *Tom Denford, CEO, ID Comms*

Praise for *BadMen* and *Laughing@Advertising*

"The Best of the Marketing Industry, 2017" *The Drum*

"New advertising classic." *Doc Searls, Author "The Cluetrain Manifesto" and "The Intention Economy"*

"It's a book that should be read by everybody in the industry" *The Independent*

"In equal parts hysterical, scathing, insightful and instructive." *Amazon Review*

"If one could write with a knife, Bob Hoffman would be the first to do so...he analyses the stupidity in business, marketing and advertising with such great humour that it actually hurts... I could not stop crying at laughing@advertising." *Amazon Review*

CONTENTS

INTRODUCTION

I was three hours into one of those horrifying 12-hour flights. The infinite expanse of the universe was visible from my airplane window but I was crammed into an area the size of a four-slice toaster. I was trying to decide whether to eat the gelatinous blob laid in front of me – playfully called "pasta" – or just kill myself. Everything in my pants was stuck to everything else in my pants. Let's just say I was cranky.

I had hours to kill and couldn't stand the thought of watching *Groundhog Day* one more time. There's a joke in there somewhere.

I took out my laptop and started reading the first draft of this book. I had reached the point in the book that I inevitably reach – where I don't know what the hell the book is about or where it's going. I decided to take a few steps back and see if I could come up with a path to glory. Or at least mediocrity.

A thought occurred to me: What have I been writing, speaking, and whining about all these years? What's the bottom line on all the verbiage I've spilled on the advertising industry? It's the simple fact that I'm skeptical. *I don't believe we really know what we think we know.*

Over the past dozen or so years I've done a lot of writing about the advertising industry. Much of it has been unflattering. This book is meant as a summary of the many things I'm skeptical about. I've drawn from my previous writing and speaking to create this compilation of grievances. I'm hoping it presents my skepticism clearly and concisely.

I suspect there are a lot of people in the ad industry who secretly agree with me but are not as irresponsible as I am and, for good reason, keep their dangerous suspicions to themselves. Maybe this book will comfort them.

If you work in advertising or marketing, or if you make decisions about advertising or marketing, I'm hoping this book will provide you with a nice healthy dose of unpopular, unfashionable opinions of the sort you don't usually get in polite company. If so, it will have done its job.

AUTHOR'S NOTES

Note 1:

I like to write short books. Publishers don't like short books. They like big fat books because it implies *gravitas*. I find the opposite. I find that most business books are about 30% information and 70% bullshit. I hate the bullshit and it causes me not to finish reading most business books. My solution is to write 30% of a book and leave you 70% extra time to enjoy a martini or bake cupcakes or whatever else you do for fun. Thanks are not necessary.

Note 2:

By the time you've finished reading this book you're going to be sick of hearing the following words: likelihoods, probability, randomness, and luck. "Likelihoods" and "probability" are very close to synonymous and I often use them interchangeably. But sometimes I use them with different nuances. "Randomness" and "luck" are also close in meaning. For the sake of clarity let me define how I'm going to use these terms:

Likelihood - the gut feeling about the chances of something happening
Probability - the mathematical chances of something happening
Randomness - surprises that occur without rhyme or reason
Luck - the amazing thing that rich people don't believe in

Note 3:

Advertising is not just one thing. There are many different types of advertising and they serve many different purposes for many different types of businesses. The focus of this book is on advertising for substantial consumer-facing brands. While some of the principles I discuss in this book are generally applicable, some are not. For example, if you make those little metal bands that connect erasers to pencils, the ideas in this book may not be for you. Sadly, nothing about advertising is either very clear or very easy.

Note 4:

I am viewing this book as a sort of distillation of everything I have written about advertising. I've borrowed extensively from other things I have written - speeches, books, blog posts, ransom notes - to cobble this together. Also, I stole ideas mercilessly from people much smarter than I.

Note 5:

One of the hardest parts of creating this book was organizing it in a coherent fashion. It became almost impossible for me to arrange the topics in a way that didn't overlap. You will please excuse me if you find some tangling of webs in the construction of the subject matter.

Note 6:

I've tried to write this so that it is useful to advertising and marketing professionals but also comprehensible to civilians. Consequently I have tried my best to limit the use of industry jargon which, if left unchecked, can turn reasonable people into demented lunatics. And, in many cases, has very publicly done so.

Note 7:

I hope you will enjoy this book. If so, any extra cupcakes would be appreciated.

"The first rule is that you must not fool yourself —
and you are the easiest person to fool."
- Richard Feynman

PART ONE: DELUSIONS

Life in fantasyland

The Lost Decade

The decade we have just experienced was expected to be one of the most fruitful and productive in the history of advertising. We had amazing new tools and amazing new media that we never had before. The whole thing was intoxicating and certain to lead to all kinds of new opportunities.

Our ability to personalize advertising and reach consumers "one-to-one" was sure to make advertising more relevant, more timely, and more likable.

Our ability to listen to consumer conversations through social media and react quickly couldn't help but connect brands more closely with their customers.

The opportunity for people to interact with media was certain to make advertising more engaging.

And yet, by the almost unanimous opinion of people inside and outside the ad business, the past decade has been the most disappointing period that anyone can recall. To wit...

- Advertising has gotten worse, not better. Rather than creating advertising that is "more relevant, more timely and more likable" we are creating advertising that is more annoying, more disliked, and more avoided. A headline in *The New York Times* recently asserted, *"The Advertising Industry Has A Problem. People Hate Ads."*

- Research indicates that regard for our industry is at a new low. It's gotten so bad we have half the trustworthiness of *lawyers!*

- Our clients don't trust us. The Association of National Advertisers (ANA) issued a widely-circulated report saying that several forms of corruption are "pervasive" in the ad industry.

- The work we're doing for brands is not succeeding. A study by Nielsen reported that consumers say they are 46% more likely to change brands than they were just 5 years ago, and only 8% say they are strongly brand loyal.

- Regulators and governments are after us with a passion. They want to know what we are doing with data and whether we are acting illegally in collecting, trading and selling personal private information about consumers.

- One study showed that of all forms of advertising, the eight types most disliked by consumers were all forms of online advertising. As a result, ad blocking apps are reportedly present on somewhere between one and two billion devices.

- Tens of billions of dollars are being stolen annually by online ad fraud.

- Our business is suffering as marketers are taking their advertising duties in-house or hiring consulting firms to do what we used to do.

- Our industry has been in the middle of dozens of scandals involving social media fraud, influencer fraud, click fraud, traffic fraud, brand safety issues and frightening abuse of data – some of which have undermined our confidence in the integrity of democratic institutions and elections.

- Consumers are becoming disgusted with our practice of tracking them, collecting personal private information about them and selling it to the highest bidder. Or any bidder at all. *The New York Times* says, *"We are living in the world's most advanced surveillance system..."*

To say that the last decade has not lived up to expectations is like saying Harvey Weinstein was a flirt.

Under the circumstances, it's hard for me to take seriously the opinions of the marketing and advertising experts who led us down this path. Skeptical by nature, I can't help but think of the past ten years as a lost decade.

The Miracle

A large part of the problem started when we advertising experts promised the business community a miracle. It was called interactivity.

It was going to be amazing. It sounded so great. People weren't just going to look at advertising, they were going to interact with it. Our advertising was going to be so much more engaging.

People were going to go online and "join the conversation" about our brands and start their own conversations and these conversations would grow and it wouldn't cost advertisers a penny. All we had to do was put up a free page on Facebook or tweet out some brilliant stuff on Twitter and we wouldn't have to waste all that money on advertising. A partner in Sequoia Capital said…*"If you can harness social media marketing, you don't have to pay for advertising any more."* It all sounded so wonderful.

But as that old sourpuss Winston Churchill once said, *"However beautiful the strategy, you should occasionally look at the results."* And what have the results been?

While people are interactivatin' like crazy all over the web, the one thing they assiduously are not interacting with are ads. In fact, display ads are usually reported to have an overall click rate of about five clicks in ten thousand ads served. If you want to know why the web is so appallingly littered with ads, it's because to get five clicks you have to run 10,000 ads.

If that's not bad enough, 60% of the clicks are reported to be mistakes. This is not interactivity. This is *absence* of interactivity. Solve Media, a company that measures this stuff, says you are more likely to complete Navy Seal training than click on a banner ad. According to research company Lumen only 9% of banner ads are even *noticed* for a second.

The idea that the same consumer who was gleefully clicking her remote to escape from TV ads was going to joyfully click her mouse to interact with online ads is going to go down as one of the great marketing fantasies of all time.

It turns out that people online react to ads in the exact same way they do offline – mostly they ignore them. Except online they ignore them with exceptional expertise. And when they do notice them, they overwhelmingly do not interact with them. Characterizing these ads as "interactive" isn't a description of consumer behavior, it's a description of advertiser delusion.

A decade ago, paragraphs like the one below from *CNN Money* were appearing everywhere.

"Imagine if Joe Smith, in need of a new car... presses a button on his remote and instantly receives more information about a Ford F150, including where he can buy one. Meanwhile, Joe's wife, Sally, watches a later ad for a Sony phone. The product on the screen is sleek and modern, and Sally wants it. She can turn her emotion into ownership, purchasing the phone with the click of a button."

Yeah, imagine if ducks played bingo.

We are living in a fantasyland — a fantasyland in which people want to engage with our "content";   a fantasyland in which consumers are clamoring for "more relevant advertising"; a fantasyland in which personalization has made advertising more appealing. It is a full-out, undiluted advertising and marketing fantasyland.

Adtech and the Long Tail of Trash

After graduating college I spent a couple of years as a middle school science teacher. There were only two problems with that — 1) I know nothing about science, and 2) I don't like children.

I also spent one year as special assistant to the Executive Director of the California Academy of Sciences. While I have no more than a layman's understanding of science and technology, I have a fascination with it. As we know, technology is neither good nor bad, it depends on how we use it. I believe that if the advertising industry had intentionally set out to use technology in the worst imaginable way, we could not have done a better job of achieving our goal.

The most extensive use of technology in advertising is called "adtech" and is used in assessing and buying media time and space. What we call adtech started simply as a computerized method for buying, selling, and distributing online advertising. It is often called "programmatic" buying, which means it is controlled by computer programs. It has morphed into a monster.

Online advertising is different from other forms of advertising in one very important way. In traditional advertising an advertiser buys advertising space from a publisher, like *The Washington Post* because they know people they are trying to reach, like Joe Smith, is likely to read it. You buy a page in the Post for next Sunday, and you can see your ad right there in the newspaper next Sunday.

Online advertising is largely bought differently. In simple terms, there's technology that knows you're looking for someone like Joe Smith. When someone like Joe Smith shows up at a website, that website sends a message to the world saying, "I have someone like Joe Smith here. Who wants him?" and an auction is held. If your technology comes up with the best bid, your ad is served to someone like Joe Smith. This all takes place in about a quarter of a second.

You often don't control where on the web your ad may appear. Your ad can appear anywhere your technology thinks it finds a person with the characteristics of Joe Smith.

The purported benefit to the advertiser is this. Instead of reaching the same user (Joe) by running your ad on *The Washington Post* website, where reaching him might cost $1, you can follow him to *somewherecheap.com*, a much lower quality website, where you can show him the same ad and it may cost you only a nickel.

Let me be careful to warn you that this explanation is an enormously simplified version of what actually goes on. I would like to offer a more precise explanation of the actual process, but sadly, no human can understand it.

In the real world, the online advertising supply chain is so replete with complexity and valueless trash that serving an ad to someone often costs tenths or even hundredths of a penny. On the surface, the value proposition of ad tech - reaching the highest value eyeballs when they're at the cheapest possible locations - is an appealing proposition.

But advertising has probably never experienced a wider gap between theory and reality. Somewherecheap.com may not actually exist. It may simply be software that looks to another computer like a website. Or Joe Smith may not actually exist. He may, once again, be software (sometimes called a bot) that looks to a computer like a person. Fraudsters have become very adept at making money by tricking the ad tech ecosystem.

If you're a fraudster and you want to create fake Louis Vuitton handbags, you have to actually make a handbag. But in online ad fraud there is no such barrier. You can create "inventory" and "Joe Smiths" out of thin air. Fraudsters can create imaginary websites and audiences from software. It's every crook's dream. There will be more about ad fraud coming later.

In general, marketers demand the lowest possible media costs. Media buying agencies have learned a very important lesson - if you are not delivering the lowest costs to your client you are in danger of losing their business. And how do you deliver low costs? By buying a whole lot of cheap ads. You may be buying bots instead of humans, you may be buying software instead of websites, but you will have very nice looking costs. The bots and fraudulent "inventory" look just like real people and real websites to many verification methodologies - and to almost all marketers. It's a con game. But a game that has been forced on agencies by brands demanding the lowest possible costs.

When a system is so complicated that its elements can't be easily understood, it is an invitation to fraud. There are hundreds of millions of low-cost, low-quality websites in the long tail of online media. It is almost impossible for major advertisers to know if the sites are real, or if their ads actually ran.

One of the by-products of the squalid and complex nature of the online advertising ecosystem is the Facebook/Google duopoly. When advertisers can't trust the system, they default to entities they believe they can trust.

Google and Facebook are known as "walled gardens." Walled gardens are online environments in which the publishers try to control our access to websites and apps. It's a way to keep us in their corral. Despite the ongoing and seemingly never-ending trail of scandals that these two companies have engendered, advertisers see these walled gardens as safe havens from the corruption and confusion of the programmatic online ad world. To some degree there is logic to this.

Walled gardens not only try to control our access to outside influences, they also have better control over what advertising appears on their sites. As a rule, they do not accept advertising from ad networks, which are generally the heaviest carriers of ad fraud. At least when you advertise on the primary Google and Facebook sites you are not subject to the same perils as you are on most ad networks. To be clear, Facebook and Google also operate ad networks of their own which *are* subject to the same "long tail trash" as other networks. But their primary sites are not part of these networks.

But Google and Facebook contain another form of peril. They refuse to adhere to the same standards of third party verification that other media adhere to. When you advertise on their sites you have to accept their word for how many people you are reaching and how long you are reaching them. To say that their metrics are not reliable is an understatement of magnificent proportions. Procter & Gamble, the world's largest advertiser, recently established its own data base of 1.5 billion people because it says it cannot trust the data it gets from Facebook and Google. Facebook recently settled a lawsuit for tens of millions of dollars in which advertisers accused it of over-representing time spent on its video content by as much as 900%.

The Context of Delusion

One last word on this subject. We poor fools in the ad business have a lot of company. A great many of the difficulties we have endured in the ad business are related to a wider misjudgment of the role the internet would play in our lives and in society.

The New York Times put it this way. The web *"was going to empower the masses, overthrow hierarchies, build a virtual world that was far superior to the terrestrial one that bound us. But the actual internet was never capable of any of that, and once it fell into the hands of plutocrats and dictators, all the gauzy rhetoric around it only served their interests."*

The utopian language of the media community at the dawn of the digital age, *"Don't Be Evil"* (Google) and *"Move Fast and Break Things,"* (Facebook) has turned out to be not so much a guidepost to a better medium, but a cautionary lesson in how quickly and easily good intentions can devolve into disturbing outcomes. It was Mark Zuckerberg who said *"I've developed a deep appreciation for how building a strong company with a strong economic engine and strong growth can be the best way to align many people to solve important problems."* I'd be curious to hear what important problems Mr. Zuckerberg thinks he has solved.

We marketers were taken in by the "gauzy rhetoric" of how the web would supercharge our efforts. The problem is we seem to have learned very little from our experience. While the rest of the world is re-evaluating the utopian nonsense it was fed about the web, we are still convinced that we are on the right path. We still allow marketing "experts" to prattle on as if the last ten years hadn't happened. We still tolerate the "we have to transform" chorus and still have no idea what we have to transform into.

We can't be blamed for swallowing the baloney that was fed to us about online advertising. But we can be blamed for having stuck to it when it became apparent it was nonsense.

PART TWO: PRETENDERS

How the changed structure of our industry turned us into pretenders

Ads Ain't Enough

We used to be pretty good at something – making ads. But making ads wasn't enough.   Advertising represents only about one-third of marketing expenditures. As our industry grew, consolidated, and went public, investors expected more than could be attained by making ads. The economics of bigness required more. They wanted more than one-third of the pie.

So we became pretenders. We pretended we were business consultants, data analysts, technology experts, digital transformation hotshots, consumer experience authorities, and masters of a boatload of other almost-advertising disciplines. We pretended that we weren't the immature kids in the corner shooting spitballs and drawing dirty pictures. And the more we pretended to be serious and moderate the more serious and moderate we became. Be careful what you pretend to be.

The sad part of all this is that there is no reason for big enterprises to be dull and stupid. Disney, HBO, and Netflix are examples of large enterprises that have maintained a high degree of creativity despite their large size. They seem to have been able to maintain their respect and appreciation for talent and creativity as they've grown bigger. We've lost ours.

They are willing to pay for talent. We are not. The large agency holding companies have allowed, and sometimes forced, experienced talented people to leave while replacing them with inexpensive unproven people. While companies like Disney, HBO, and Netflix get into bidding wars over experienced proven talent our industry throws talent away every day.

For decades we have been accused of being too airy-fairy and of not having measurable, tangible criteria for creativity. Our reaction has been to overreact and become "data driven" instead of idea driven. We have lost confidence in the creative process and would rather invest in activities that yield charts and graphs that our clients can understand. Ideas and creativity are too ethereal. We can't measure them, so we have devalued them.

Today, we are mediocre at a lot of things and not very good at anything. We are a floor wax and a dessert topping. We are confused about what we do and why we do it. For years every expert in the advertising and marketing pantheon has been lecturing us on the need for transformation. The only thing they haven't been able to tell us is what we should transform *into*. Every change we've made seems to have made things worse.

We've had a lost decade. We have allowed ourselves to be bamboozled by the suspect assertions of articulate people – and more than a few clowns – masquerading as experts. We have lost any healthy degree of skepticism. It has cost us dearly.

As our industry has evolved, the scope of our pretensions has evolved.

This chapter is about pretending. It's about pretending we know things we don't really know. It's not about the creative kind of pretending that imaginative children do. It's about the destructive pretending that misguided adults do.

Reality Is a Mess

We think we know how the world works, but we don't.

Until a few years ago, we thought we knew what the universe was made of. There was matter, which at our scale was largely atoms composed of electrons, neutrons, and protons (and lots of other tiny sub-atomic things bouncing in and out of existence.) And there were four forces - gravity, electromagnetism, and the strong and weak nuclear forces. It turns out that we were wrong. In fact, we have no idea what the universe is made of. Science now believes about 96% of the universe is "dark matter" and "dark energy." Which is another way of saying we have no clue what the hell it is.

In *"The Cooling World,"* April 28, 1975 Newsweek magazine informed us that meteorologists *"are almost unanimous"* that *"catastrophic famines might result from…global cooling."* On Sept. 14, 1975 The New York Times told us that this global cooling *"may mark the return to another ice age."* And on May 21, 1975 the Times said *"a major cooling of the climate is widely considered inevitable"* because it has been *"well established"* that the climate in the Northern Hemisphere *"has been getting cooler since about 1950."*

It seems that although they were "almost unanimous" and it was "well-established" and "inevitable" meteorologists, too, were apparently wrong.

For about 25 years I took an aspirin tablet every day because it was good for my heart. But a few months ago the medical community announced that we should stop taking aspirin every day because not only is it not good for us, it's bad for us.

This is not to say that we don't learn from science. We continually do. But at every discrete moment of history we have deluded ourselves into believing we knew things that we didn't really know. If the A students who study physics, cosmology, and medicine are so often wrong, do we really believe that the C students who go into advertising know anything?

In some fields experts have credibility. Mostly it is in fields of hard science where expert opinions can be tested. In soft sciences, like economics and sociology, where enormous variables exist and controls are hard to establish, experts have far less credibility. Not because they are any less serious, but because their theories are difficult to prove or disprove. There is also far less agreement within these disciplines. A quote attributed to George Bernard Shaw goes like this, *"If all the economists were laid end to end, they would not reach a conclusion."*

Sadly in the field of advertising and marketing, experts are not usually hatched based on their record of producing reliable results, but on their ability to attract attention. As Nobel Prize winner Daniel Kahneman says, *"a reliable way to make people believe in falsehoods is frequent repetition."* Consequently we should be highly dubious of their "expertise." But we're not.

Our delusions are not just about the material world. They are also about ourselves, our abilities, and our nature. These delusions live inside us and color everything we do. They infect our opinions of who we are. They distort our place in the world, twist our behaviors, and warp our sense of reality. Like the proverbial fish in the ocean, we are so immersed in delusions we can't even sense they are there.

We are very good at filtering out information that does not fit neatly into our vision of the world. *"We can't cope otherwise,"* says James Glieck, author of *Chaos,* and biographies of Newton and Feynman.

The business of marketing is particularly rife with delusions. We think we know how advertising works. We think we know what will motivate people and what will not. We think we know what tomorrow is going to be like. And yet every day we unconsciously ignore significant evidence that contradicts our most cherished beliefs about how advertising works, how media works, how marketing works, and how people work.

- A few years ago it seemed there was a law that that required us to include *"Like us on Facebook"* or *"Join the conversation"* in every ad we created. Today if you put *"Like us on Facebook"* or *"Join the conversation"* in an ad you'd be laughed out of the conference room.

- In 2012, the Harvard Business Review published a piece that purported to quantify the value of a Facebook "like." Here's the formula:

$$V = L / UpM \text{ x } (LpD \text{ X } 30) \text{ x } (C/L) \text{ x } CR \text{ x } ACV$$

It is now several years later and we know the true formula for the value of a like:

V = o

In fact, Facebook has begun to experiment with phasing out the "like" button.

- After months of research and testing we create advertising that has little to no effect. Despite this we continue to believe in the research and testing methodologies. Early in my career we wouldn't even think of airing a tv spot unless it got a certain score on a "Burke" test. Anyone who questioned the Burke methodology was considered a fool. Today, if you suggested a Burke test you would get a hearty chuckle and a cold shower. Advertising delusions live as religion and die as punch lines.

- For almost twenty years we have measured the effectiveness of online advertising by click-through rates (CTR.) Reliable studies show that CTRs have little to no correlation to ad effectiveness, yet it is still the most widely utilized measurement (or Key Performance Indicator, in ad jargon) of online advertising performance.

- In 1996, marketing expert Seth Godin had this to say to Fast Company..."*I guarantee you that by the year 2000, Internet banner ads will be gone.*"

- We discount the effects of luck and random occurrences on our efforts. The tourism people in Australia created a terrific campaign called "*Matesong.*" As Mark Ritson says...'*Matesong' was a wonderfully executed bit of advertising. A big idea. A great score. An amazing backdrop… And then the fires came."*

We go into new business presentations and make bold, cocksure statements about our own particular brand of dubious advertising philosophy. And we never have the guts or self-assurance to tell the truth – that our posturing is just a guess at likelihoods and probabilities.

Part of it is our fault. We are not willfully deceitful. We just find it very hard to admit that we are devoting so much of our energy and our soul to something about which we understand and control so little. Part of it is the environment. Our paymasters want results. They don't want to hear that they are buying millions of dollars of likelihoods and probabilities.

Advertising is chock full of contingencies and unintended effects. There are a multitude of critical steps in the development of strategy, creative concepts, media plans, production, and spending alternatives. None of which assures success but every one of which can foreshadow failure. Something as routine as the casting of a model in a photo shoot can have an enormous effect on the success or failure of a campaign. And that's just one of a hundred variables. We cannot possibly assess or control all the variables in a methodical way. So we fall back on our delusions and our vague notions of how advertising works. In other words, we pretend.

The workings of the real world are impossibly complex and disorderly. As Glieck says, we *"prefer to turn a blind eye to reality's messiness."*

We Don't Know What We Think We Know

I've been around advertising a long time. I spent over forty years in the business and another six or seven writing about it. I've noticed something. I've noticed that we advertising experts have a lot of unreliable opinions.

I'm a good example. I had a long and pleasant career in the advertising business. I've been the CEO of three ad agencies. I had the opportunity to create campaigns for brands like McDonald's, Toyota, Bank of America, Chevrolet, and AT&T. I've been invited to speak in dozens of countries. My opinions and comments have been sought by organizations like the BBC, The Wall Street Journal and other substantial media outlets. I've written four books about advertising that were each Amazon number one sellers in the category. Marketers have literally spent hundreds of millions of dollars based on my advice. I don't say any of this to brag. I say it for the exact opposite reason — to make an important point:

I don't know anything.

I am faking it. I always have been. I have no idea why anybody buys anything. I have no idea why you buy Coke instead of Pepsi, or Nike instead of Adidas. As a matter of fact, I have no idea why *I* buy Coke instead of Pepsi. As we used to say in my hometown of Brooklyn, I don't know shit.

In my career I've worked with hundreds, if not thousands, of marketing and advertising people. They were mostly intelligent, well-meaning, hard-working people. I mean no disrespect, but I don't think they knew shit either. I think we pretend to know a whole lot of stuff that we don't really know.

What we do mostly is precision guessing. We guess. We know what other companies have done, we understand their strategies and their methods. If it worked for others we try something like it ourselves and hope it's going to work for us. We have a fancy name for this. We call it "best practices."

But the problem is, every company is different, every problem is different, every brand is different, and every circumstance is different. And what makes best practices in one instance may be a total disaster in another.

Often what we do works a little. It works a little because we spend a lot of money on it. If you spend enough money on media you can make questionable undertakings seem providential. Every now and then something works amazingly well and we don't know why, but we pretend it was because we're really smart. Sometimes we are. Sometimes we're lucky.

There are so many variables in advertising and marketing, and our individual successes and failures provide such a small sample that it's hard for us to know what is the result of our acumen, and what's the result of — I don't know — luck, circumstances, trends, randomness... something else?

I've had enough advertising successes and failures to know that I never knew what was going to be successful and what was going to flop. No matter how much I thought I knew, I never really knew.

There's a guy named Ron Johnson who was head of retail stores for Apple. He pioneered the Apple store — the most successful stores in the history of the world. After several years he was hired away from Apple by JC Penney. Johnson applied all the lessons and all the successful strategies he had used at Apple to JC Penney. Everyone expected an enormous success. He created one of the most colossal failures in the recent history of American business. In his final quarter as CEO of Penney their sales dropped an almost impossible 32%. If we gave my dog Roscoe an office at JCPenney headquarters and made him CEO and let him lie around and drool all day, he could not lose 32% of sales in one quarter.

Johnson was clearly a brilliant guy. And he applied all the knowledge and experience he had used at Apple. But like all of us, he didn't know what he thought he knew.

It is not only history that misleads us. The future also misleads us. If you attend a lot of conferences as I do, you have undoubtedly noticed that speakers love to talk about the future. In fact, it's almost the only thing they ever talk about. Why? Because the present is too confusing, too complicated and largely incomprehensible. But the future is great. You can't be wrong when you talk about the future. No one can fact-check the future. You can say anything you want and people will think you are brilliant. They will applaud you and quote you in the news.

And then 10 years from now when it turns out you were wrong, who cares? Nobody remembers.

Advertisers spend half a trillion dollars a year on advertising. You'd think they'd know their business. But there is convincing evidence that they are alarmingly out of touch.

Thinkbox, the TV trade organization in the UK, commissioned a study a few years ago comparing advertisers' assumptions about consumer media behavior with the facts of consumer behavior.

First, they asked marketers and agency executives how many minutes a day they thought people spent watching video on demand. The ad experts said 81 minutes. The actual number was 8 minutes. The experts were off by 900%

They asked how many minutes per day people watched subscription video on demand like Netflix. The experts said 84 minutes. The actual number was 11. The experts were off by over 600%

They asked how many minutes a day the average person spent with YouTube. The experts said 62 minutes. The correct number was 16. Off by almost 300%

Advertisers in the U.S. are equally misinformed.

A study released in 2016 showed that among U.S. advertising and marketing executives when asked what percent of video watching time was spent with television, they said 25%. The actual number was 82%

They were asked what proportion of video viewing was done on a smart phone. They estimated 18%. The answer was 2%. Wrong by 800%.

The obvious question is this – how can people who work in an industry that is constructed on media behavior be so astoundingly misinformed? Every day tens of millions of dollars are committed based on the supposition that these people know the facts and are spending money wisely.

People in our industry are misinformed to a degree that is startling. There are a few reasons for this. One reason is that advertising people live in a different world. If you need evidence, have a look at this table from a few years ago, comparing UK advertisers' social media and online behaviors to that of real people. If you had any doubt that we live in a different world from our customers, this ought to clear it up.

Percent Engaging In Various Online Activities

	Advertisers	Real People
LinkedIn	93	14
YouTube	92	60
Facebook	90	62
Twitter	81	22
Netflix	63	30
Amazon Prime	30	15

A while back I was making a presentation to a large advertising group in a country that I will not name so as not to embarrass the hosts of the conference. I was reviewing my presentation with the hosts and going through the information quoted above about how wildly misinformed agency people were about media behavior. One of the hosts begged me not to include the numbers in the presentation. Yes, she stated, we know how misinformed the advertising community is, and yes, she said, we understand how it is hurting us. But if we publicly tell the agency people how terribly wrong they are about media behavior there will be an awful backlash against us.

The advertising and marketing industry would be wise to keep open minds and admit that a great deal of our understanding of consumer behavior is incomplete at best, and wrong at worst. We would do ourselves and our industry a whole lot of good by exercising a little modesty and discretion when we claim to know things we don't really know.

Our Principal Problem

In most fields of endeavor progress is achieved by the accretion of knowledge over time.

In medicine, for example, we learned of the germ theory of disease. Then we learned that germs were spread by dirty things like flies, mosquitoes, and sex. But it all started with the basic knowledge that diseases weren't caused by frogs or witches, but by germs.

In aeronautics, the materials we use to make airplanes are completely different from the ones used 100 years ago. But we still use the same fundamental design of a fuselage and a pair of wings. The principles of air travel are over 100 years old (sadly, so is the food) but the principles are still being built on.

Copernicus taught us that the universe did not revolve around the Earth, but that the Earth revolved around the sun. Then we discovered that there were other bodies revolving around the sun. Then Newton figured out the mechanism for all this - gravity. One discovery leads to another.

Advertising is different. We respect no history. We observe no principles. We have no connective tissue. Every generation tosses out what was learned before and declares it dead. Marketing is dead. The "big idea" is dead. Positioning is dead. Brands are dead. The funnel is dead. Traditional media are dead.

Every generation invents its own dreadful jargon that for a brief time passes for wisdom – likeonomics, engagement, conversations, storytelling, empowerment.

The absence of verifiable principles is the dirty little secret behind why we engender so little respect in the business community. Well, that and Gary Vaynerchuk.

In most disciplines there are unifying principles. Some examples: Physics has the law of conservation of energy. Biology has natural selection. Economics has supply and demand. These are fundamental to the nature of the endeavor. In advertising, what are the proven unifying fundamental principles that we all accept? If there are any, I don't know what they are. A field of endeavor without principles is not a discipline – it's a free for all.

We used to believe that creativity was the essence of successful advertising. No so much anymore. We used to believe that big ideas were the backbone of outstanding advertising. Not so much anymore. We used to believe that an agency's primary job was the delivery of outstanding ads to its clients. Not today.

What do we believe in now? Likeonomics, engagement, conversations, storytelling, and empowerment? These aren't principles. These are the dreadful clichés of a tired industry.

Advertising's Arrow of Progress

One of the interesting aspects of advertising that I have tried to explore from time to time is whether we should think of it more as art or science.

With the growth in the use of technology, mathematics, metrics, and data it appears that certain aspects of advertising are becoming more scientific. However, I am not convinced that advertising as a whole is any more scientific.

From a practical standpoint, there is one factor that differentiates art from science. In science, there is an "arrow of progress." As described in the previous piece, science points in a direction and gets progressively more specific and effectual.

If you buy a new car, it is more likely to last longer, be safer, work more reliably, and be more efficient than it was fifty years ago.

If you have high blood pressure today, you are more likely to be successfully treated for it than you would have been fifty years ago.

If you have a personal computer, it can do more things, more effectively, more quickly and more reliably than it did fifty...wait a minute...we didn't have personal computers fifty years ago.

The point is, science provides us with technological progress by degrees that builds on itself and improves stuff. Art, on the other hand, does not have an arrow of progress. It's not supposed to. Art is about human interpretation – emotions and aesthetics – not ongoing improvements. You want to improve on Mona Lisa? Good luck.

There is no way to talk about whether the work of Picasso represents "progress" from DaVinci. You may prefer one to the other, but to speak about progress is meaningless. Similarly, is there an arrow of progress from Beethoven to James Brown? Or Shakespeare to Updike? One may certainly have influenced the other, and styles certainly change, but talking about improvement is moot.

That doesn't mean art isn't inventive or innovative. Or that older forms don't influence newer forms. It just means that art moves unsystematically and, unlike science, we don't judge new art based on having improved upon old art.

So the question of whether advertising should be considered more science than art rests on answering this question: Is there an arrow of progress? In other words, is advertising more effective and more successful at its objectives than it used to be?

Exploring the literature of advertising over the past ten years, one would have to conclude that advertising is *less* effective, not more. The literature is rife with assertions and research that conclude that advertising's effectiveness seems to have diminished over time.

There are certain aspects of advertising that claim to utilize scientific principles more effectively – media planning, programmatic buying –

but there isn't much in the way of conclusive evidence to support the idea that advertising as a whole has gotten more effective.

In fact, despite all the hoo-hah over the precision targeting of online advertising, behavioral targeting seems to be only marginally more effective than no targeting at all. It is not clear that when the marginal effect of behavioral targeting appears, it is even due to advertising. It may well be that the reason behavioral targeting sometimes appears to be more effective is that the people who are being targeted have been so carefully pinpointed that they are the most likely people for buying the product, regardless of advertising.

Economists call this the "selection effect." The selection effect posits that the appearance of more effective advertising can be a mirage that is caused by the targeting of people who were already more likely to buy, click, or download your product.

But even if we stipulate that certain aspects of advertising have become more scientific, I would still contend that the overarching goal of advertising – the creation of successful brands – is no nearer to a scientific practice than it was when I entered the advertising business thousands of years ago.

From what I can see, despite all the technology we have applied and all the words that have been written, we have uncovered no new generally accepted principles about the nature of brand building or consumer behavior. Most marketers are still thrashing around in the dark trying to either build a brand or maintain one.

Regardless of the growing veneer of scientific processes, there seems to be no arrow of progress that has helped us understand how to create more successful advertising.

PART THREE: HERESIES

Waste Not, Grow Not

The Fame Game

If you're 6'10" there's no guarantee you'll play in the NBA, but it's a hundred times more likely than if you're 5'10".

If you graduated from Stanford there's no guarantee you'll make a good living, but it's a hundred times more likely than if you dropped out of high school.

If you look like Melania Trump there's no guarantee you'll get a job as a weathergirl, but it's a hundred times more likely than if you look like Angela Merkel.

It may not be fair, or right, or pretty, but it's true.

So if you're 5'10" you better have a Plan B. If you drop out of high school, you better have a skill. And if you're Angela Merkel, forget the weather and shoot for Prime Minister.

In advertising, as in life, there are no certainties. There are just likelihoods. There are no true-false questions or yes-no answers. Just probabilities.

I spent over forty years in advertising and marketing and in that time I saw very little evidence that people who are supposed to be experts in the field of consumer behavior had any idea of the importance that probability plays in the work we do.

The reason this is important is that marketers will spend months torturing strategies, arguing over adjectives in briefing documents, and analyzing type faces on websites, while ignoring the most *probable* avenue to marketing success: Fame. You are massively more likely to be successful if you're famous.

I sat in advertising meetings for decades (some seemed to last for decades) and watched my clients argue over the most mundane and meaningless trifles about competing campaign ideas and never once even consider the most important aspect of the entire endeavor — which of these ideas is most likely to make us famous?

Fame is a monstrously huge advantage in business.

If your brand is famous, retailers are far more likely to put you on their shelves, distributors are far more likely to pay attention to your calls, consumers are far more likely to buy your product, people are far more likely to serve your product to their guests, guys are far more likely to wear caps with your name on it, important people are far more likely to invite you to lunch, answer your emails, and meet you for a drink. And smart people are far more likely to want to work for you, be your lawyer, or sit on your board.

But fame has a problem. It is not an elegant concept. It's too simple, crass, and obvious. It is not abstruse enough for most advertising and marketing executives. They get published and become "experts" by creating arcane theories of consumer-brand relationships. They earn their stripes by taking the obvious and making it incomprehensible. They get their jobs by convincing CEOs and other erudite fakers that marketing is mysterious and that understanding consumer behavior is a very complex and cryptic business. They think they know the mind of the consumer and how to manage it. And in doing so, they jump right over the most obvious and likely route to success.

Before we go any further, let me emphasize that fame by no means *guarantees* success, but it makes it massively more likely. You might say it's essential but not enough.

Is Coca-Cola any more refreshing than Bob's cola? Does a Nike t-shirt make you a better athlete than a Bob's t-shirt? Does an iPhone sound any better than a BobPhone? Not in any world I've inhabited.

Yes, there are certainly product differences. And yes, some products are demonstrably better than others. But as an advertising person you have no control over that. You're stuck with the job of selling more of it regardless of its quality.

In all the incessant jabbering about marketing, and all the strategic gymnastics that marketers put themselves through, the simplest and most obvious objective of marketing should be to create fame. Brands that are famous have an enormous advantage over brands that are not famous.

I have disappointing news for most brand managers, planners, and strategy directors. The refined strategic insights you struggle to achieve are mostly lost on consumers. First, they don't notice them and second, if they do notice them, they rarely matter much. Sorry. Our bold insights may seem compelling in the friendly confines of the conference room but out there in the grocery aisles, showrooms, and retail sites the stringent logic of the conference room is often irrelevant.

The world's largest, most successful brands – the Apples, Nikes, Cokes, Pepsis, Toyotas, McDonald's, Tides, Budweisers, *et al*, all have one thing in common – they're very, very famous.

At this point I am sure that there are some annoying pettifoggers looking for holes in this argument. They will say it's circular. "It's not the fame that's causing success, it's success that's causing fame." That argument is good for about 30 seconds until you realize that each of these brands spends about a zillion dollars every year to *remain* famous.

I have no idea what the dollar impact of fame is. Maybe it's large, maybe it's just moderate. But whatever it is, multiply it by seven billion people every day, and you get a sense of its power.

The problem is that fame is not easy to come by.

There are several ways for brands to achieve fame. Some do it by being clearly superior and generating exceptional word of mouth. This is obviously the best way to become famous. In the beginning, this is how Google achieved fame.

Some get lucky. They're good copy. The press loves to cover them, follows them everywhere, and provides them with zillions in free exposure. As I write this Tesla is the most valuable car company in the history of the world by market value. They spend very little on marketing. But they are constantly in the news.

Uber and Facebook are other examples. In their formative years these brands spent very little on marketing but there were times when it was hard to open the business section without finding references to them. Facebook was the subject of a movie. With very moderate marketing expenditures these brands became enormously famous.

Others become famous through imaginative PR initiatives, clever stunts, the charismatic personalities of their leaders, or a combination of these things. There are many ways to achieve fame.

Sadly, positive word of mouth is wonderful, but rarely manageable. The likelihood of the press falling in love with you is one tick above zero. Imaginative PR is invaluable but very hard to come by. And charismatic leaders are one in a thousand and, let's be honest, usually assholes.

The most expensive way to become famous is through advertising. It is the most expensive, but also the most reliable. It is the only avenue to fame that you can buy your way into.

The Simple-Minded Guide
to Marketing Communication

Before we take the subject of fame any further, let's take another side-track into likelihoods and probabilities.

As mentioned above, we marketing people have a dreadful habit of taking the obvious and making it incomprehensible. So I would like to go against the grain and take the obvious and make it *more* obvious.

Earlier I asserted that the advertising industry has few if any generally accepted principles. So I would like to offer up a few. If you are someone who has to make decisions about how to spend marketing dollars, here are some principles for simplifying and clarifying your decision making.

The first thing you have to understand is that when making communication decisions your first job is to assess likelihoods and probabilities. In other words *precision guessing*. You need to reckon which of the many alternatives you are faced with has the highest probability of producing the result you are looking for within the budget you have. You must also recognize that assessing likelihoods and probabilities is a ridiculously difficult job. We think we understand the variables, but never fully do. We never plan on randomness. We never factor in luck.

A second principle is to understand the limits of what we do. We don't have as much power to create business greatness as we think we do. There are too many important aspects of business success that are out of our control. We don't control the product; we don't control the pricing; we don't control the distribution; we don't control the employees – we only control the message. We have to be realistic about the limits of what the message can impart to a poorly made, badly designed, overpriced, hard-to-find product. Or a product with any one of those characteristics.

Third is perhaps the most obvious. Brands that are *in the spotlight* have a much higher likelihood of being successful than brands that are not in the spotlight. This is where we have leverage. For this reason alone all marketing communication should have a common objective – to *find a piece of the spotlight.*

This is also one of the reasons that our industry's current obsession with precision targeted, personalized advertising is misguided. Personalization and precision targeting may be valuable for certain types of marketing activity like direct sales and niche marketing, but have a very low probability of producing fame for major consumer facing brands. Building a big brand requires the widespread attention - fame - that one-to-one advertising does not generally provide. Precision targeted, "personalized" communication has a low likelihood of delivering widespread attention. Do you think Donald Trump would have become president if *The Apprentice* had been a webinar?

As mentioned previously, there are many ways to attempt to find the spotlight. First, you have to lose your delusions. You are not going to become the Amazon of anything, the Google of anything, or the Facebook of anything. It has a minuscule probability of happening for you. Most of us have to *think* or *buy* our way into the spotlight.

Once you decide on your strategy, there is one other principle you must employ. There is nothing that creates a greater likelihood of attaining high visibility than *creativity*. The probability of your efforts shining a light on your brand is enormously higher if you have an imaginative idea behind it. I will say it again - regardless of which communication or media strategy you employ, there is nothing more likely to garner you a piece of the spotlight than a great idea.

So let's recap:

- Your most under-acknowledged job is assessing likelihoods and probabilities.

- You must be realistic about the power of advertising

- One of the most essential characteristics of a successful brand is high visibility *i.e.*, fame.

- One of your strategic imperatives is to produce fame and visibility by garnering a piece of the spotlight.

- Achieving a place in the spotlight is extremely difficult.

- You are more likely to attain the spotlight by being widely seen rather than narrowly focused.

- Splitting hairs over words in briefing documents is largely a waste of time. Most of the distinctions you draw between your brand and your competitors are lost on consumers. A much more productive discussion is, *"Which strategy or execution is most distinctive and has the highest probability of making us famous?"* In the long run, the strategy with the most value for your brand is the one that is most likely to buy you high visibility.

- A key question you must answer is whether you have the assets to achieve a piece of the spotlight? The assets that have the highest probability of garnering that are *money* and *creativity*. There is rarely enough money.

As a simpleminded guy, all of this seems obvious to me. However, our industry appears to be in such a state of confusion that the obvious is no longer credible.

Please do not send me your favorite example of a big brand that was built outside the lines of these principles. Of course there are some. There are no rules, just likelihoods and probabilities.

Public Advertising vs Private Advertising

Among the obsessions of the digital age of advertising has been the drive for personalization. It is taken for granted that the more personalized an ad is and the more precisely it is targeted, the more effective it is likely to be. There are very few in our industry who question this assumption. And yet, it is highly questionable.

The proponents of personalized advertising tell us that one-to-one, precision targeted advertising is far more capable of performing successfully because it reaches "the right person, at the right place, at the right time." This may be true if your goal is to generate a click. For this task personalization and precision targeting may be an effective technique. However, if your goal is to build a brand, I have seen no evidence that this is true. In fact, I have seen considerable evidence to the contrary.

There are several cogent arguments for not accepting the idea that personalization and precision targeting are superior to generalized strategy and mass reach. In arguing against personalization, I'm going to radically summarize (I hope without misrepresenting) a few ideas on the subject proposed by people other than (and smarter than) myself.

Rory Sutherland, Vice Chairman of Ogilvy, UK points out that fame imparts singular benefits on people and companies. At the most basic level, people are more likely to choose famous products over unknown products. Let's do a little thought experiment.

You've been driving all morning on a two-lane highway and you're getting hungry. You come to the small town of Nowheresville and at the intersection there are two hamburger joints. One is McDonald's, the other is Bubba's Burgers.

It is likely that Bubba makes a better burger than McDonald's. But it is also more likely that you will choose McDonald's. Why? I think the answer goes something like this.

While you might like to have a better burger, it's more important that you don't have a *terrible* burger. While you might like to stop at a place that is comfortable and relaxing, it's more important that you don't stop at a place that *is gross* and has six months of dried snot stuck to the bottom of the table.

McDonald's may not make a great burger, and it may not be the most elegant environment, but you have a reasonable expectation that the burger won't make you sick and the tables have been cleaned. In other words, Bubba's may very well make a better burger, but McDonald's is good enough, and relatively risk free. The aversion to risk trumps the possibility of incremental superiority.

So the question is, why do you believe McDonald's is good enough and safer? I think the answer is simple. McDonald's is famous. The underlying logic is that famous brands *can't afford* to be too dangerous or gross.

Another way of understanding the value of fame is called signaling. In a paper in the Journal of Advertising Research, December 2004, by

Tim Ambler and E. Ann Hollier entitled, *"The Waste In Advertising Is The Part That Works"* Ambler and Hollier describe the value of signaling.

Here's my example. I walk into a room. I ask everyone to please be quiet. I announce, *"I just want you all to know that I am the sexiest man in the world."* I have said one thing but signaled another. I have said I am the sexiest man in the world but I have signaled that I am a giant asshole. The argument that Ambler and Hollier make is that mass targeted advertising is also a form of signaling. Regardless of the message, it tells the world that you are a substantial company, that you have deep resources that are underpinned by success, and that you believe in your product enough to spend large sums of money to support it. As Doc Searls describes it, *"it is akin to a male peacock's fanned-out tail. It speaks of the company's substance, and the fact that it can afford to advertise."* And do it widely.

A third reason to question personalized advertising is described as "cultural imprinting." This is a term invented by Kevin Simler. The logic supporting his cultural imprinting idea is that in some way we all want to be part of what is culturally acceptable.

As he says, brand images are *"part of the cultural landscape we inhabit. They provide cultural information. When we ignore brand messages we're missing out on valuable cultural information and alienating ourselves from the Zeitgeist."* He says this puts us in danger of becoming outdated, unfashionable, or otherwise socially hapless. We become like *"the kid who wears his dad's suit to his first middle school dance."* In other words, in some way brand choices send messages to others about who we are. And no one but a sociopath wants to send the wrong message.

So what does all this have to do with the personalization problem? In Simler's words *"cultural imprinting relies on the principle of common knowledge. For a fact to be common knowledge among the group, it's not enough for everyone to know it. Everyone must also know that everyone else knows it."* In other words, part of our purchasing calculation is not just our belief that X is an acceptable product, but our expectation that *other people* believe X is acceptable because *they know what we know.*

In mass media, I know what my friends are seeing. I know that if they're watching football they're seeing the same ads I am. Consequently I have reasonable confidence that my friends believe that Nike makes acceptable running shoes, Ford makes acceptable pick-up trucks, and Heineken makes beer I don't have to feel weird about.

But I have no idea what my friends are seeing online. If we all live in our own little personalized, one-to-one digi-world, I have no frame of reference for "cultural imprinting." I don't know if my friends will think me an idiot for buying these headphones I saw advertised on *somewherecheap.com.*

In a nutshell, this may very well be why thus far mass-market advertising is demonstrably more effective at brand building than highly personalized advertising. Highly individualized, personalized advertising makes advertising a more private, rather than public experience. It creates uncertainty as to what advertising our friends are seeing. Which in some way keeps us from knowing what brands may be culturally acceptable.

To a significant degree, mass media is public advertising, and personalized one-to-one advertising is private advertising. If you're a brand marketer and you want to grow, you have two choices. Be wasteful or be invisible.

It's hard to become famous in private.

The Wrong Math

You might expect that the claim of superiority for personalized one-to-one targeting would be met with skepticism. For one thing, there is very little record of it having achieved much. Shouldn't we exercise reasonable skepticism about a theory for which there is not much evidence?

All of our huge brands – Apple, McDonald's, Coca-Cola, Toyota, Budweiser, Tide, Crest, Nike, etc. – have been created largely by the supposedly wasteful and sub-optimal mass media. But the power of the marketing feedback loop seems to have caused our industry to lose its ability to be sober or skeptical.

The reason we accept the story of "mass one-to-one" with no evidence is that *a)* big mouths are talking about it, and *b)* our math experts (in media and data) say it's true.

I don't believe the experts, but I do believe in math. I believe math can offer us insights into how advertising works and how consumers can be influenced. The only problem is, I think we're using the wrong math. If you'll pardon my cliché, we have the wrong algorithm.

I don't know what concept of math the data experts use to persuade marketers that "one-to-one" is the media model of choice, but I believe the math model we should be using is *probability*. In other words, which media strategy is most likely to produce the desired result? There is ample evidence that broad-based media has the highest likelihood of achieving the desired result of building substantial brands, and very sketchy evidence of any other type of advertising doing so.

The mathematics-based rationale for the primacy of mass one-to-one advertising and its alter ego, personalization, seem to go something like this: *a)* by "personalizing" you are not wasting money on people not interested in your product, and *b)* customized ads are more relevant and persuasive.

This may be true for certain types of B2B marketers, direct response marketers, and highly-specific brand categories. But I think these rationales are wrong for mainstream brands.

Byron Sharp tells us the key to growing a brand is acquiring new customers. I believe probability tells us that the more people we communicate with loudly and in public the more customers we are likely to acquire.

Rory Sutherland says *"A flower is just a weed with an advertising budget."* His point is that flowers expend a lot of resources to look and smell pretty out loud and in public. About 125 million years of evolution have shown that the expenditure pays off. If there was a superior way for a rose to attract bees by individually targeting certain types of bees with certain types of attractors one would assume it might have evolved by now. Instead, roses produce a lovely, fragrant flower and let probability do its work.

Date vs Probability

I took my data analyst with me to Las Vegas.

We spent three days at the roulette wheel. We learned *thousands of little things*. We did a thorough, highly detailed analysis of what went on:

- We counted how many times red came up and how many times black came up.
- We calculated the effect of the croupier spinning the ball left or spinning it right.
- We calculated how often red came up three times in a row. Then black.
- We established the effect of the speed of the roll on the number of times it turned up red or black.
- We computed the number of people over 40 at the table and how that affected the result
- We checked the wind direction and how that affected the roll of the ball
- We counted and analyzed tons of other stuff.

We lost anyway.

Meanwhile the house did no data analysis. But they knew *one big thing*. They knew there were 38 numbers and they paid 35 to 1. So they had a 5% advantage. Over time, they never lost.

In marketing and advertising we have two ways of doing things. We can measure every little data point or we can see the big things.

Small picture advertisers know a lot of little things:

- Who went to what website?
- What they searched for.
- What kind of car they drive.
- Who their dentist is.
- Where they bank
- And tons of other stuff

They create tightly focused advertising and put it in front of a select number of precisely targeted individuals.

On the other hand, *big picture* advertisers know a few big things:

- People are more likely to buy brands that are famous.
- People are more likely to buy brands that make them feel good.
- People are more likely to buy brands they like.

They work very hard to produce *widely appealing materials* and put them *everywhere they can*. Then they stand back and let probability do its work.

Why have all the world's leading brands been built by big picture marketers? Because the more you study data, the more you realize that probability is data writ large.

What if Targeting Doesn't Work?

I have a basement full of oddball ideas about advertising. Some of which concern areas in which I have no credentials or expertise. I've never bought a dollar's worth of media in my life, but that doesn't prevent me from having firmly-held, ill-informed opinions. So here come a few of my heretical views on media buying.

One of them is that "media science" may be a little science and a lot of hooey.

What if all the targeting we do is mostly unnecessary complexity masquerading as knowledge? What if there are only one or two important pieces of data we need when planning media to make it most efficient? What if the cost of further targeting exceeds the benefits it provides?

What if the only really important thing we need to know when planning media is whether a person participates in our category? If we're selling golf balls, the only important targeting question we have to ask is, "Does this person play golf?" If we're selling wine the only important question to ask is, "Does she drink wine?" If we sell tires the only important question is, "Do they own a car?"

All the other stuff – their education, their income, their weight, height, and serial number, their zip code and psychosexual predelictions, the websites they visited yesterday, and the number of chickens in their backyard – may be interesting, but what if they don't do a damn thing to make our media buys more effective?

During my semi-brilliant advertising career I would never have suggested such a thing to a client. Clients don't like oddball ideas. They are resolutely devoted to believing what everybody else believes. And everyone else believes that leveraging data to create precision targeting is the future of advertising.

There is actually some science to back-up my heresy.

- According to research conducted by a professor at MIT, a fellow at the Melbourne Business School, and the Head of Operations and Technology at Group M, data that is informing your programmatic ad buys may not just be unproductive, it may be counterproductive. In one test, data bought from a data broker was able to correctly intuit the sex of an individual 43% of the time. A cat flipping a coin would be right 50% of the time.

- A second test of data acquired from data brokers improved targeting performance by 184%. Sounds good right? The only problem is that acquiring that data... *"creates extra costs of about 238% on average in comparison to random placements."*

- Dr. Augustine Fou says that by using just three data parameters (gender, age, location) you may already be eliminating 98% of the population. What's left when you use 100 data parameters instead of 3 and you've eliminated 99.99%? Are you left with real people, or "lookalikes," or just plain baloney?

I'd love to see an advertiser do a split run. In one market buy media based on the usual   demographics, psychographics, data-o-graphics, graph-o-graphics, and bullshit-o-graphics.

In another matched market run the same campaign but make the media buy based on just one behavioral criterion – does the person participate in our category or not?

I'd love to see the cost-benefit results.

Reconciling Sharp and Ritson

I'm much more interested in the creative side of advertising than I am in the marketing and media parts. But there are a couple of marketing people I pay particular attention to. They are Byron Sharp and Mark Ritson.

They are both professors and both work in Australia (since I wrote this, Ritson has left academia to concentrate on his private sector pursuits.) Sharp wrote *"How Brands Grow"* which is a wonderful marketing book and probably the most influential of this era. Ritson is one of the most entertaining, outrageous, and sensible speakers and writers on marketing you'll ever come across. Unlike me, they're not just bomb-throwing blowhards. These guys actually know things.

They agree on a whole lot of stuff regarding the clown show that is contemporary marketing. But there's one thing they disagree on – the value of segmentation and targeting. At the risk of mischaracterizing their positions, let me be clear that these are *my words and interpretations*, not theirs.

Sharp thinks that in mass marketed consumer product categories segmentation and targeting are often empty exercises. Ritson thinks that segmentation and targeting are one of the essentials of marketing.

Sharp's argument is that for mass marketed brands, growth is a function of how many customers you can acquire, and that the best way to acquire as many customers as possible is to advertise to as many people as possible. He does a good job of convincing us that one of the attributes of leading brands is that they have a long tail of *light* users. He asserts that the best way to acquire a long tail is by talking to everyone.

Ritson argues that no one can afford to reach everyone efficiently. He would say that without segmentation and targeting, strategy becomes dangerously nebulous and media dollars get sprinkled lightly everywhere instead of focused where they can do the most good.

I'm somewhere in the middle.

I'm a big believer in mass media. But my experience in the real world of agency life taught me that this is often not practical, and that somewhere along the line the reality of budget constraints will interfere with the desire to talk to everyone. In other words, every budget restriction becomes a *de facto* targeting restriction.

So the key issue is what is the most efficient way for a major brand to use advertising dollars to acquire new customers? I believe the answer is somewhere in between their positions. To the extent possible mass media should be utilized. But it should be tempered by a bias toward targeting heavy users *in the category*.

So when targeting and segmentation are employed they should be based on behavior, not demographics, psychographics, or any other thing-o-graphics.

As Prof. Sharp points out in his book, heavy users in a category tend to be promiscuous - they often use several brands in the category. Heavy fast food users tend to be customers of several fast food outlets. Heavy wine users tend to buy lots of different types and brands. Consequently, there is plenty of opportunity to attract new users to your brand from within the segment of the population that is already active in the category.

For example, the dominant brand of soft drink in the U.S. is Coca-Cola. But Coca-Cola only has about an 18% share of market. This means that 82% of the time people who drink soda don't buy Coke.

It seems reasonable to me that the best use of one's advertising money is to spend it against the component of the population that likes and participates in the category but has not been converted to your brand. This is an argument in favor of segmentation.

However, it's not that easy to identify these people because in mass marketed categories like soft drinks they tend to be widely dispersed throughout the population. In this I agree with Sharp. While I would love to spend all my ad dollars focused on actual soda drinkers, and particularly heavy using ones, it's hard to see how you can put up a billboard that is only seen by these people.

That leaves me in between the two professors. To me, the usefulness of segmentation and targeting have been oversold, but are still valuable. But the idea of spending money against light or non-users has also been oversold.

If, as Prof. Sharp asserts, heavy category users tend to be promiscuous, I would suggest that acquiring a long tail of *light users for your brand* is best achieved as a by-product of targeting the frequent users in your *category*.

It seems that this hypothesis could be easily verified or refuted by studying the category habits of light *brand* users. In other words, is the long tail of light Coke users comprised mainly of light or non-users of soft drinks or frequent users of soft drinks who are not regular Coke users? (Professors, have at it.)

While finer segmentation and targeting may be useful in niche categories and B2B, I believe for most mass marketed products there are only a few important segmentation distinctions that provide significant value and they are mainly behavioral. You will certainly sell more lipstick by targeting women rather than men, but once you make that cut I suspect the returns of further segmentation diminish rapidly.

Sharp and Ritson are wonderful examples of how the contradictory theories of brilliant people can exist side by side and still both be valuable and convincing. It's one of the apparent contradictions that makes advertising endlessly fascinating.

PART FOUR: LOST

Misguided ideas that have infected our industry

Check Your Logic at the Door

As business people we are taught to think logically. The logic of business is mostly quite simple. If I do A then B will happen. In other words, it is the logic of cause and effect. For most business activities cause and effect is the right way to think.

It is not the right way to think about advertising. The right way to think about advertising is likelihoods and probabilities. Advertising is too unpredictable and too contingent to assign anything like the assumed reliability of cause-and-effect. I pompously call this the "quantum advertising" effect.

Until the discovery of quantum theory in the early 20th century, scientists were convinced that there was a logical cause-and-effect explanation for all physical phenomena. They might not understand a given phenomenon at the moment, but given the right tools, the right methodology, and enough time, they believed they could derive a logical explanation.

This was undermined by quantum theory which asserted that there are no certainties — just likelihoods and probabilities. Among other weird things, it asserts that something can actually change by the process of being observed. The idea that observation could change the nature of something was completely radical and deeply upsetting, but has turned out to be true. Look at it one way, it's a particle. Look at it another way, it's a wave. Look at it at all and it will change from a wave to a particle. If you've never read about the mind-blowing "double-slit experiment," I suggest you do so.

The point is that business people, like scientists, are used to thinking that there is a logical explanation for every business phenomenon. We may not know the answer now, but given the right tools, the right methodology — you may substitute the right metrics and the right data — and enough time, we can find a logical explanation for all consumer behavior. I'm not so sure. The idea that more data will lead us to a universal understanding of how advertising motivates an individual consumer may ultimately result in our arriving at the same conclusion we have reached about the physical world – it is way stranger and way more complicated than we imagined.

On the other hand, if we think about advertising in the context of likelihoods and probabilities, consumer behavior is much more easily understood. Consumers are more likely to buy products they are familiar with; they are much more likely to buy products that are easy to buy; they are much more likely to buy products they believe are socially acceptable; they are much more likely to buy products that make them feel good.

As we sit here today, we have two major competing models of consumer behavior. The first model suggests that consumer behavior is basically logical. This theory asserts that people behave rationally and do not throw their money away on stupid crap. There is a lot of persuasive evidence for this model. A good example is in retailing. Retailers know that they can stimulate sales by lowering prices, offering discounts, and utilizing other types of promotional activities. This is clear evidence for a rational basis for consumer behavior.

The second model asserts that consumer behavior is essentially non-rational, or emotional. This theory, brilliantly demonstrated by Daniel

Kahneman, holds that people are not really aware of their motivations and are influenced substantially by emotions or subconscious activity. The evidence for this model is equally persuasive. In my career I have witnessed the story of the Toyota Corolla. It was the exact same vehicle as the Chevy Geo Prism, built in the same plant by the same people on the same production line. The only difference was the name. It cost $ 1,500 more, yet outsold the Prism 3 to 1.

So we are faced with a problem. We have contradictory models of consumer behavior that both seem to be valid - the rational model and the emotional model. Either there is another model which we cannot see underlying them both, or we need a more comprehensive explanation that unifies the two. In quantum physics an elementary particle can be understood as either a particle or a wave. I am going to suggest that in advertising, consumer behavior also has a dual character.

In quantum physics there are no certainties – just probabilities and likelihoods. I am going to suggest that in advertising our strategies have no inevitability about them. Just probabilities and likelihoods. On the nature of light, Einstein said:

"We are faced with a new kind of difficulty. We have two contradictory pictures of reality; separately neither of them fully explains the phenomena of light, but together they do."

I believe this type of duality and uncertainty is true in advertising and marketing as well.

- Under certain circumstances, a brand can be described as having great power with a consumer. And in certain circumstances the same brand may have little to no effect on the same consumer.

- The same person may buy brands whose advertising she likes, as well as brands whose advertising she hates.

- The same person may buy products that are clearly differentiated, and products that are generic.

- The same person may buy bargain products that are exceptionally good values, and luxury goods that are ridiculous and overpriced. I am convinced that many people who bought Gwyneth Paltrow's famous $75 "This Smells Like My Vagina" candle also saved 39¢ by buying bargain peanut butter the next day.

This is not unusual. In fact, this duality is typical of consumer behavior. There is an inherent contradiction that confounds us and mocks our most cherished beliefs about individual consumer behavior. I'm going to invent an obnoxious term here, but it's necessary to communicate what I'm trying to say. The term is "behavior plasticity."

The point is that because of the duality of consumer behavior, marketers who think they can describe it as either this or that are wrong.

"Behavior plasticity" – or the duality of consumer behavior – is the most mysterious and confusing element of marketing. It is the one factor that marketing people continuously misunderstand in their struggle to describe and predict individual consumer behavior.

Believing in the orthodoxy of one advertising philosophy, one media philosophy, or one creative philosophy is a trap that misreads the fascinating subjects of both advertising and human behavior.

Advertising's Untold Stories

Have you ever wondered why the highly touted marketing miracles you read about in the press never seem to work for you?

In recent years, copywriters, branding experts, strategic thinkers, and advertising and marketing agencies have evolved a conceit by which they refer to themselves as "storytellers."

Although it is largely self-inflating bullshit, I enjoy this conceit. It puts an emphasis on the concept of stories and helps me explain and expose one of the great logical errors of our industry. I call it the "untold stories" problem. Here's how it works.

Most of the information we get about the success or failure of advertising and marketing initiatives comes in the form of a story:
- A press release
- An article in a trade publication
- A feature in the business section of the news or on a TV business report
- A case history presented at an industry conference or event

The stories that reach us are often superficial – they are mostly just headlines lightly dusted with a few specifics, some meticulously curated numbers, and a generous helping of spin. This is because marketing strategies are valuable trade secrets and keeping them confidential is crucial to business success. You don't just give 'em away. As a result, the narratives we get are often devoid of some important specifics that are key to understanding the true nature of the "story."

Nonetheless, for every story to which we are exposed, there are a thousand untold stories we don't get to read or hear about. These are the non-spectacular stories, created in non-spectacular fashion, by non-spectacular brands. In other words, they are about 99% of everything that ever happens in marketing.

I don't think it's terribly controversial to suggest that we are far more likely to read success stories than failure stories. Ask any business reporter. The number of PR releases she gets about a brilliant new campaign being launched will outnumber the releases she gets about the dismal failure of a campaign by about a zillion to one.

After all, who wants to alarm the Board, embarrass the CEO, scare the shareholders, and frighten the puppy dogs by revealing what bewildered bumblers they are? It's a lot wiser to be forthcoming about your successes and circumspect about your failures.

When this becomes terribly dangerous is not when it is applied to a *specific* case history, but when it is applied to primary information we get about *marketing fundamentals.*

I would wager great stacks of money that the untold stories of the mediocre performance of virtually all marketing activities outnumber the widely circulated stories of success by a hundred to one. This is doubly true of (but not limited to) the trendy shiny-new-object activities like social media, content marketing, virtual reality, native advertising, "personalization," and whatever new marketing miracle happens to be trending this week.

The narratives we are exposed to about these marketing activities, and the belief we have in their efficacy, are profoundly skewed by the bias toward trumpeting success, not failure.

This is perilous. It leads to conferences, books and, god help us, webinars, extolling the effectiveness of marketing activities based on *wildly unrepresentative samples*. It gives our entire industry a false impression of the value of these undertakings.

It leads us to throw money at expensive, wasteful tactics. And it reinforces the lemming-like attraction of naive marketers to the trendy fantasies that have dominated our industry for the past decade.

It is not that the stories themselves aren't true. It is that the results being reported may be wildly divergent from the results to be found in the total number of stories on the subject, the vast majority of which go *untold*.

Before you take any report about advertising or marketing as indicative of a general truth, you'd be wise to assume that just the fact that it is being told *at all* makes it likely that it is one or two standard deviations from normal. You should assume that the overwhelming number of stories that *haven't been told* on the subject are not nearly as rosy.

In marketing, the untold stories are usually the *real* story.

More Elephant Advertising

In a *Wall Street Journal* op ed piece, Mark Zuckerberg had this to say…

"People consistently tell us that if they're going to see ads, they want them to be relevant. That means we need to understand their interests. So based on what pages people like, what they click on, and other signals, we create categories…online advertising allows much more precise targeting and therefore more-relevant ads."

Zuckerberg's VP of "Global Marketing Solutions" says all the surveillance and tracking that is going on is *"good for people because it gives them more relevant advertising"*

If you want to know how these grifters come up with this "more relevant advertising" baloney, let's talk about a little research trick that devious operators use to con gullible rubes. I will give you a small silly example which I hope will make it clear on a large scale. It goes like this.

Let's say you want to open a strip club in a residential neighborhood. No one in their right mind wants a strip club in their neighborhood. But as the potential owner of the strip club you have to make a case to the city council to get your permit.

You do a survey in your community. What you *don't* ask is a direct question, *"Do you want a strip club in your community?"* because you'll get a resounding no and a few solid kicks to the golden globes.

Instead, you ask a question that *sounds* like a suitable question: *"Do you think the residents of Nowheresville would benefit from more recreational and entertainment opportunities?"* This question has a couple of benefits to the strip club promoter:

- Who is going to say no to the vague notion of *"more recreational and entertainment opportunities?"*
- The so-called *"recreational and entertainment opportunities"* are not defined

Once the survey is completed you go to the city council and show them your pitch slides:

- 88% of people in our community are in favor of *"more recreational and entertainment opportunities."* That's what we provide!
- We understand that not everyone will be in favor of our business, but enjoying our shows is entirely voluntary and no one is forced to patronize our establishment.

Even a city council isn't dumb enough to buy this horseshit. Even a city council understands when they're being conned. That's how they're different from us.

I would submit to you that this is *exactly* the type of specious rationale that underpins the claims of the adtech industry that people want "more relevant advertising." This claim is put forth virtually every time the creeps and spymasters are asked to justify their surveillance practices. But, like the strip club study, it's based on flim-flam.

By posing questions in manipulative ways that don't actually describe the issues in question, it is easy to use research to distort the truth. If you ask someone "do you prefer ads that are relevant?" of course they're going to say yes.

But if you ask the proper question — *"Are you willing to trade private, personal information about yourself and your family, have your movements tracked and catalogued both online and offline, have your emails and texts scanned and archived, and have files about you sold to anyone who wants to buy them, in order to get more relevant advertising?"* — I don't think you need to be a research genius to know what the answer will be.

How Brand Advertising Became Synonymous with Bullshit

It has become a generally accepted truth in the marketing industry in recent years that we are too focused on short term results and not focused enough on brand building. Field and Binet have done excellent work to demonstrate this. Everyone from Byron Sharp to Martin Sorrell has commented on it.

Despite our recognition of this issue, we continue down the destructive path of short-termism. A recent article by Mark Ritson bemoaned this. Ritson included some data showing that short-termism is not just continuing, it's accelerating.

"Its incredibly depressing to see that this trend of short termism is not just going to continue, it's getting worse," said Prof. Ritson.

If we know that continued investment in short-term tactics at the expense of long-term brand building is counter-productive, why do we continue to do it? Some of the reasons are obvious:

- The brief shelf-life of a CMO: When your life expectancy is measured in months, there is little incentive for you to think in years.
- Short-term activities show instant results: And there's nothing that C-Suite meatballs and restless toddlers like better than instant results.
- Brand building efforts yield soft measures: Even if you're doing a great job of brand building, how do you prove it to accountants?

Indications of brand strength are not the measures that impress CFOs or Boards. They want sales data, and they want 'em now.

- The web: Online advertising has become the dominant form of advertising and it has been used mostly as a short-term or direct response sales medium. As Tom Goodwin says, *"Why has there never been a brand built with digital advertising? There are many answers, the main one is that we've never tried to."*

But there is another reason for our discomfort with so-called brand building activities, and no one likes to talk about it. In some circles "brand advertising" has become synonymous with bullshit. And, sadly, in too many cases it *is* bullshit.

Our industry has frittered away substantial credibility by allowing anything that doesn't have a cogent sales message to be excused as "brand" advertising. Much of what we call brand advertising has become squishy and free of discipline. We've become flabby and self-indulgent.

Sadly, brand advertising has come to mean pretty much anything we can put a logo on. There is almost no frivolous marketing activity that can't be excused as "branding." Put your logo on a pair of socks? Branding.

In reality, there are two kinds of things we call "brand" ads – those that are specific to a product and actually help sell something, and those that are someone's hobby horse with a logo pasted on at the end. The unfortunate part is that our dreadful vocabulary defines them both as the same thing – "brand" advertising. They are not.

I'm sorry but pretty pictures and a nice track are not enough. Pounding your chest for world peace is not enough. Buying a pop tune and having people jump around is not enough.

Successful brand building is difficult work and requires advertising that says something. Ads that build brands best are those that have a clear and specific message about a product and deliver it in a memorable way.

Just because your ad is image heavy and free of a sales message doesn't mean you're brand building. Not selling is not enough.

True Detective: How Bullshit Becomes a Fact

There is so much bullshit in our business that sometimes you have to wonder where it all comes from. A while ago I decided to "peel back the bullshit" and see if I could reconstruct how something that was completely wrong wound up being represented as a fact in reputable publications like *Forbes* and *The Drum*. Here's the story.

Samuel Scott, columnist for *The Drum*, called out his publication in a tweet quoting some nonsense from an opinion piece that appeared in that publication.

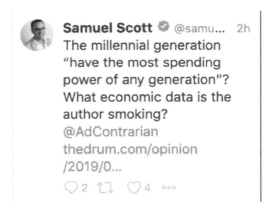

Anyone with half a brain knows that millennials are nowhere near having the most spending power. People over 50 control 70% of the wealth in the US, and are responsible for about half of all consumer spending.

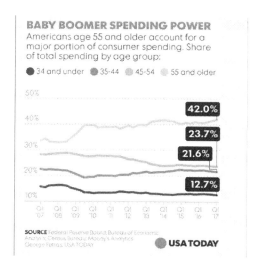

In fact, as the chart above shows, on a per capita basis millennials have the *least* spending power of any adult group.

So I decided to do a little detective work and try to figure out where this bullshit "fact" came from. In doing so, I got a nice close-up look at the astounding ignorance and sloppiness that is embedded in our industry, and how bullshit, repeated with enough frequency, becomes a fact.

I started with the aforementioned piece in The Drum. It was called *"Why Direct-to-Consumer Companies Are Using Influencer Generated Content to Win Over the Market."* It was a thinly disguised self-promotion piece full of the usual influencer hysteria. As noted above, the piece claimed that millennials *"have the most spending power of any generation."*

To justify this claim, the article linked to an article in *Forbes* entitled *"How To Tap Into The Millennial $200 Billion Buying Power With*

Social Media" which asserted that *"By 2018, they will have the most spending power of any generation."*

The article offered no back-up for this claim other than a link to something called *"41 Revealing Statistics About Millennials Every Marketer Should Know."*

The *"41 Revealing Statistics..."* piece lived on an agency website, always famous for their assiduous pursuit of accuracy. It was written by someone who was two years out of college and called herself a "Marketing Strategist." The two-year-old marketing strategist had this to say about millennials...

8. They will have the **most spending power of any generation** by 2018. (Bazaar)

Once again, there was no back-up for this claim other than a reference to something called *"Bazaar."* Searching for Bazaar lead me to a PDF from 2012 entitled *"Talking To Strangers: Millennials Trust People Over Brands"* by a company called *Bazaarvoice* that sells some kind of software for harnessing the power of "user generated content."

Once again, there was no detail or proof, just this assertion...

It's true. By 2017, Millennials – currently in their mid-teens to mid-30s – will have more spending power than any other generation.[1]

The attribution for this claim was a footnote that referenced a book...

1. Kit, Yarrow and O'Donnell, Jayne. Gen BuY: How Teens and Twenty-Somethings Are Revolutionizing Retail, 2009.

This book was published in 2009 and was one of those "millennials are a new species" things that were all the rage until it turned out that millennials were pretty much just like everyone else, except younger and poorer. What I found in the book was this...

"Generation Y, (remember when 'millennials' were called Generation Y? -BH) those born between 1978 and 2000 has overtaken baby boomers in sheer numbers and is poised to do the same with its incomes by 2017..."

Of course, this turned out to be completely wrong. Millennial income did not overtake baby boomers in 2017. According to *Business Insider*, in 2018 in the U.S. millennials trailed baby boomers in income in every state in the union...

"In all 50 states and Washington, DC, the median millennial made less money than the median Gen Xer or baby boomer...The gap in median income between millennials and baby boomers ranged from the older generation making about 25% more than millennials in Iowa to 65% more than millennials in Alaska."

The average millennial income is about $35,000. The average baby boomer income is about $46,000. There are about 9% more millennials than baby boomers, but their income is about 24% less. So even though there are substantially more of them, in aggregate their income is way behind baby boomers.

Here's a graph that demonstrates that income per capita among baby boomers is far higher than millennials.

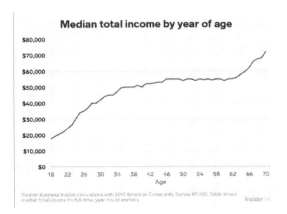

One more thing. Even if millennials had higher income than baby boomers, that still doesn't mean they would have "the most spending power." Spending power is not just a function of income. It is a function of income plus accumulated wealth plus access to credit. According to the Federal Reserve, baby boomer wealth is more than 15 times that of millennials, which means they also have enormously more access to credit.

So let's recap the timeline and the trail.

- In 2009, a book incorrectly predicted that millennial income would surpass baby boomer income by 2017.

- In 2012, in a self-promotional PDF by a software company, this false prediction was used to assert that millennials would have "more spending power than any other generation" by 2017.

- In 2017, a piece of "content" on an agency website, written by a two-year-old "marketing strategist" used the quote from the software company to assert that millennials "will have the most spending power of any generation by 2018."

- Later that year, an article in Forbes referenced the agency website to justify a claim that, "By 2018, they (millennials) will have the most spending power of any generation."

- And recently, in 2019, an article in The Drum leaning on the fiction in Forbes, proclaimed that millennials "have the most spending power of any generation."

And that, my friend, is how in the slovenly and slipshod world of marketing, bullshit becomes a fact.

The Millennial Hustle

While we're on the subject of millennials and bullshit, it would not be an exaggeration to say that for much of the past decade the marketing and media industries have been obsessed with the new species of human called millennials — the poor bastards born between about 1980 and 2000 — who have been credited with and blamed for everything that's right and wrong in contemporary society.

Here's a quote from *Time* magazine:

"This generation has no fantasies...today's youth appears more deeply committed to... decency, tolerance, brotherhood — than almost any generation...What (this generation) possesses in every stratum is a keen ability to sense meaning on many levels at the same time...Today's young are committed as was no previous generation to redeeming... social imperfections."

You would not be unwise to assume that the quote was about millennials. But it was not. It was from Time's *Person of the Year* 1967 — today's much maligned baby boom generation.

Researchers, media, and marketing experts have been selling us the exact same generational twaddle for over fifty years now, and we dimwits keep buying it.

Here's how it works. If you want to be a successful consultant or marketing guru you must first convince the hysterical and the gullible (that's us!) that things are changing dramatically and they are in dire danger of becoming irrelevant if they don't understand the new type of human that is now changing the world. The only way to stay ahead of this curve is to rely on...hmm, let's see...Us!...and our proprietary knowledge and expertise about this new species.

So every fifteen or twenty years they invent a new generation that's completely different from the last. They have distinctive, mysterious characteristics that only the deeply connected and erudite (that's Us!) can explain.

It's all bullshit. It's astrology. How can you possibly take an enormous component of the population — tens of millions of people — and say they all have this or that characteristic? The absurdity is thrilling.

Jennifer Kriegel has written a book about the myth of generational stereotypes. Kriegel was writing her doctoral dissertation on *"the unique attributes of the millennial generation"* when she discovered something. It was all nonsense. Instead what she discovered was *"how remarkably similar the generations are."*

Here's Kriegle, *"There are a million factors that go into determining the kind of person you are when you grow up, and this arbitrary 20-year-long age bracket is not one of them... characteristics often attributed to millennials...are...merely attributes of various life stages."*

If you're a marketer I have an interesting thought for you. There is just as much diversity within generations as there is between generations.

Blaming the Click

There was a time when advertising was thought to be some kind of freakish, annoying art form. Now it's just freakish and annoying. In an effort to make it more efficient, the "art form" seems to have been squeezed out of it. What happened? And why has advertising lost its dubious status as the black sheep of the art world?

I have a theory. I blame the click.

Except in direct response advertising, before we had the click we never had a unit of advertising value. Individual ad value was largely a subjective matter. It was measured over time in either sales growth or brand growth, but individual ads themselves were hard to value directly. We were not capable of giving them a quantitative value in discrete units of measurement.

The click changed that.

As online advertising became the dominant form of advertising, and as the click became the key measurement of online advertising effectiveness and the key currency of online economics, we came to believe in the religion of clickonomics.

Advertising students were trained to think in terms of click effectiveness. They were taught to develop strategies and executions that maximized demand generation, customer engagement, and sales traffic — which mostly turned out to be just fancy terms for clicks.

This was reinforced when they got out of school and into the real world of advertising. Their work was evaluated largely on the basis of how many clicks it generated. The fact that clicks were shown to be a false proxy for ad effectiveness was largely ignored. In a world in which measurement was worshipped, even false measurement was better than no measurement. Soon the ad students who were trained in clickonomics were in charge.

Frank Zappa's explanation of how the music industry became a shit show is a pretty perfect description of what happened next in advertising...

"What we had then was fat old guys with cigars who didn't know anything about music and didn't care. We came to them with a new sound they said: 'I don't like it but I hate this shit anyway, maybe the kids will like it. Try it, if it sells we'll go with it, if it doesn't, we'll can it.'

So what happened was lots of experimental stuff got made, lots of new stuff, sounds you never heard before.

But then they began hiring young guys who liked the music and thought they knew all about it. If we came up with something new, these young guys would say 'I don't like it, and I know a lot about music. We're not putting that record out. Go and do something I like.'

And that's what's ruined the music industry. You've got people who think they know, people who think they're experts. So they kill everything that doesn't conform to their opinion. That's why everything sounds the same, because these young guys are everywhere now."

I'd say that's a pretty excellent description of where the ad industry is. I would love nothing more than to see advertising returned to its shaky status as a freakish art form. Even a black sheep is better than no sheep.

Our dismal standing with the public should be enough to wake us out of torpor. But sadly the industry is currently in the hands of *"...people who think they know, people who think they're experts."*

Pokémon Went

In 2016, the *American Marketing Association* published an article entitled, *"How Pokémon Go Is Disrupting Marketing As We Know It."*

Advertising Age went with *"A Marketers Guide to Pokémon Go."*

The normally ultra-sober Wall Street Journal ran *"Ad Agencies Scramble To Form Pokémon Go Strategies."*

Marketing Week gave us *"Why Pokémon Go Is A Game Changer for Augmented Reality And Marketers."*

Other advertising and marketing publications gave us these headlines...

"How Brands Can Leverage the Pokémon Go Craze — And What They Can learn From It"

"How To Use Pokémon Go For Marketing"

"Marketers Look To Climb Aboard The Pokémon Go Phenomenon"

and my personal favorite...

"Is Pokémon Go The Future Of Digital Marketing?"

Why devote any space in this book to Pokémon Go? Because Pokémon Go is the embodiment of the idiotic obsession the advertising and marketing industry has with miracles and shiny new things.

Pokémon Go lasted about a half hour as a cultural craze and about 10 minutes as a marketing miracle, but the culture that created Pokémon Go marketing hysteria has spanned a decade.

I would love to be able to give you a firm accounting of how much money has been wasted in the past decade on obsessions with blockchain, virtual reality, millennials, "content", 5G, Pokémon Go and every other flavor of miracle the industry became temporarily obsessed with.

But we never learn. In our world, wisdom has been replaced by trend spotting. The people most highly regarded in our industry are not those with the best record of creating success, but those with the best fairy tales about "what's coming next." We have become an industry of idiot futurists who think we can predict what's coming tomorrow but seem to be completely blind to what's happening today.

My Social Media Paradox

I am a social media success story who is highly skeptical of social media. A few years ago I was invited to speak at a social media conference. The hen was in the fox house. My presentation was billed as a "fireside chat" between the organizer of the event and myself.

The first question he asked went something like this...

HIM: You have been critical of the social media marketing world from the get-go, yet you use it... quite well I might say. What's your point of contention and how can you reconcile that with your prolific use of the medium?"

I thought it was a great question. I don't remember my exact words. So here's a combination of how I think I answered the question and what my subsequent thoughts have been.

ME: Let's start with why you invited me here to address this conference. There are hundreds of advertising and marketing people who are skeptical of the claims of social media marketers. I am not alone. But for some reason you chose me. Why? Let's answer this question in marketing terms.

I would suggest that the reason you chose me is that I have created a pretty successful brand called *The Ad Contrarian. The Ad Contrarian* brand is clearly differentiated. When you needed a "product" in my category (someone to add controversy and piss people off) you knew what brand to "buy."

The interesting thing, as you mentioned, is that whatever success I have had in building this brand has been done mainly through the use of social media. Why then am I so vocal in my criticism of the social media industry?

The first part of the answer is that having accomplished the most difficult of marketing tasks - building a brand - I know how difficult it is. I know how hard I have worked at it. And knowing this, I am outraged when I have to listen to or read the idiotic nonsense of fakers posing as social media experts. Until they have created a successful brand using social media *themselves* they have no credibility with me.

Social media is very hard work. Very few social media programs have anything resembling significant sales impact. Virtually every company in the country now has some kind of social media program in place. Every organization, club, charity, band, team, corporation, and poker game has a blog, website, podcast, Facebook page, or Twitter feed. A miniscule proportion of them have any impact on the world. So when I hear social media "experts" promising the moon, I get infuriated.

Additionally, all the nonsense I read about "content" makes me sick. I know how difficult it is to create "content" that anyone gives a shit about. I have spent every day of my life for the past 10 years creating "content." I know first hand how difficult it is to break through the billions (literally) of web pages and online noise to get anyone to pay attention to what you have to say. When I hear idiots pop-off with their facile clichés about creating "compelling content" I know they have no idea what they're talking about

I also know how many billions of dead blogs, inactive Facebook pages, lifeless Twitter feeds, and rotting YouTube videos there are out there in the digi-dumpster. I know how many billions of carcasses of "content" are lying around like a decaying lox.

The idea that consumers want to interact with brand content is the grand delusion of the social media set. They think because athletes, movie stars, and pop singers have millions of followers people are interested in engaging with pencil, mayonnaise and paper towel sellers.

I come at social media as someone who has had far more success with it than most of the "experts." I have used social media successfully and have accomplished more with it than most of them will ever accomplish. I have used social media to create a brand and sell a bunch of books. The only thing most of these "experts" have created is a powerpoint presentation.

The second part to my answer is this. In addition to being a reasonably successful social media "entrepreneur," I also had a little $100 million ad agency which I ran.

I don't think there are too many social media entrepreneurs who also ran an ad agency. I don't think there are too many agency CEOs who are also social media entrepreneurs. Consequently, I think it is fair to say that I have a reasonably unique perspective.

So when I hear digital hustlers and social media phonies shooting their mouths off about how advertising is dead, and television is dead, and marketing is dead, and everything else that isn't online or social is dead, I want to expose them. That is, after I strangle them.

They are clowns and charlatans. They are undermining the credibility of the social media industry and they are causing damage to their clients.

My experience has proven to me that social media can be a valuable marketing tool. But it is not magic, it is not a miracle, and it cannot and will not replace everything that came before it. So, yes, despite the fact that I have used social media very successfully, and although I know there are lot of talented and hard-working people in social media, I have a healthy amount of disrespect for a large segment of the social media industry.

Whatever Happened to "The Conversation?"

We're over 10 years into the era of social media and I think it's time we took a step back and had a fresh look.

The fact that social media is a huge cultural phenomenon is very interesting. But it is only relevant to marketers insofar as it affects our ability to influence consumer purchasing behavior or the building of brands.

It's also time to be precise about what we mean when we say "social media." Our first chore is to separate "social media" from "social media *marketing*." We are not sociologists, we are marketers. We know that social media has been a huge worldwide phenomenon. But how about social media *marketing*? How effective has it been for the purpose of advancing product sales and building brands?

This is a critical distinction and has been at the root of tremendous misunderstanding and incalculable misuse of marketing dollars.

When the idea of social media first was introduced, it seemed impossible that it wouldn't have massive value in marketing. The logic went something like this: People are going to use social media to talk with each other. They are interested in brands. They will surely have conversations with and about brands. The web will allow them to share their enthusiasms with others who will, likewise, pass these conversations on and potentially create a huge amplification in which a few comments can morph into literally tens of thousands of impressions.

As Facebook CEO Mark Zuckerberg put it in 2007...

"The next 100 years are going to be different for advertisers starting today... For the last 100 years media has been pushed out to people, but now marketers are going to be a part of the conversation."

Of course, the attraction to marketers was instantaneous and powerful – who doesn't want to create tens of thousands of positive impressions without spending a cent in media? In fact, many proclaimed the advent of social media to be the death knell for traditional advertising. Understandably, marketers quickly adopted social media marketing as a fundamental component of their marketing activities.

Just as every now and then a relief pitcher hits a home run, inexorably a few brands did some things with social media that became big commercial successes. These successes became legendary and were offered up at every conference, in every magazine, and at every new business pitch as evidence of the remarkable power of social media. As time went on, however, it became clear that the philosophical foundation of social media marketing was flawed. People were enthusiastic about engaging with their friends on social media by sharing personal experiences, political opinions, silly videos, photos of children, pets, and meals. People were excited about connecting with athletes, movie stars, and pop singers. But they seemed to demonstrate little or no interest in talking with or about most brands — except to gripe about mistreatment.

But we became really good at ignoring the evidence of our own eyes.

A look at any Facebook page or Twitter feed would have quickly convinced any dispassionate observer that people were *not* broadly sharing their enthusiasms for brands. In fact, people were overwhelmingly *not* voicing enthusiasms for brands at all. And on the rare occasions when they did, their comments *did not* often get shared and go viral, but quickly trickled away.

Additionally, pages that brands built on Facebook and feeds they created on Twitter drew initial interest as novelties, but soon became moribund as consumers found them to be bland and self-serving.

Becoming a publicly held company, and needing ways to make money for its shareholders, Facebook saw what was happening and quickly changed its tune. To their credit, Facebook pulled one of the most amazing bait-and-switch jobs in the history of business. Notwithstanding Zuckerberg's earlier proclamations, they realized they were in the *traditional advertising sales* business. They dropped the fancy talk about "conversations" and quickly started to "push" ads "out to people" in astounding and unprecedented numbers.

Facebook's business is no longer about providing a forum for conversations about brands. It is now believed that about 1% of a brand's followers receive that brand's posts organically. As Forrester Research vice-president Nate Elliott has said...

"Any marketers who believe they're having a conversation on Facebook are delusional"

Remarkably, there are still marketers and agencies who believe — or, in the case of some agencies, pretend to believe — that spending ad dollars on Facebook is "social media."

It is no such thing. It is *traditional paid advertising*. But, as always, the social media lobby is nothing if not cunning. Every time their spurious claims are exposed they redefine "social media" to fit the facts. So we now have "social ads" – a complete contradiction in terms. The companies that were supposed to *replace* traditional paid advertising are now the *world's largest purveyors* of traditional paid advertising.

Social media is an amazing worldwide phenomenon. But social media *marketing* — and the promise of free lunch through conversations and sharing — has turned out to be a fantasy.

Prisoners of Youth

After World War II something new arrived in the U.S. – the teenager. Previously, in all of history, there was no such thing. For centuries there were just young people who went out in the fields or down in the mines or over to the factories and worked their asses off. Overwhelmingly, the fruits of their labors and the imperatives of their lives were focused on the relentless struggle to keep themselves and their families alive. It was a brutally hard existence.

That changed over time. By the 1950's and 60's, unprecedented prosperity and affluence arrived and the "teenager" was born. A teenager was a young person who had what no other young person in history ever had – money and time.

With the teenager came something else that was completely new – youth culture. At first it was just music and language. But then a whole set of customs and values evolved including fashion, celebrities, attitudes, economics and imagery.

Coincidental with the rise of pop culture was the rise of the "creative revolution" in advertising. In the beginning, advertising didn't have much use for pop culture. Have a look at the great ads from the early period of the "creative revolution" (VW, Alka-Seltzer, etc.) and you'll see the ads were about *products* not "*lifestyles*," the actors were grown-ups, and youth iconography didn't exist.

Slowly but surely youth culture worked its way into the advertising lexicon. At first it was thrilling. Young people were tickled to hear their favorite types of music and see people like them in ads. What made it exciting was that it was new and different.

Fifty years later, advertising has become tethered to youth culture in a way that is undermining imaginative thinking, harming our creative output, and seriously limiting marketing effectiveness. Youth culture and fashion have always been stupid. If you want to die an imbecile, don't pay attention to art, literature, history, science, or nature. Pay attention to Kardashians.

What has changed is that pop iconography is no longer the exception in advertising. It is now by far the dominant tool in the tool box. Pop culture is no stupider today than it was 50 years ago, it is just more pervasive.

And that's a problem. As wealth and economic power have been hugely concentrated in the hands of mature people, youth culture rarely interests or engages the people who have and spend most of the money. In fact, it is often off-putting. But it has become the default language of advertising despite the fact that it is not the language of the people who drive our economy or dominate our commerce.

Worse, it is self-perpetuating. The more that marketing people see youth-orientation dominate advertising the more they unconsciously assume that it is the proper voice for advertising and that they better employ it, too.

As a result, much of advertising has become a tiresome, one-note exercise in celebrity/music/technology banality. It creates a false feedback signal to marketers and the business community that pop culture/youth sensibility is the correct vocabulary for marketing.

There is nothing wrong with the use of celebrities or cultural trends in advertising so long as they are not used as shallow substitutes for ideas. Once, a small percent of advertising leaned on pop culture as a replacement for creativity. Today that tactic is much more prevalent. The constant drum beat of music/celebrities/technology is everywhere and the wonderful surprise of unexpected, off-the-wall, illogical advertising is largely missing in action.

We are tethered to youth culture in a way that is harmful to our goals and to business. The attribute most noticeable in creative work is not imaginative thinking, it's the slavish conformity to whatever's trending. As usual, our obsessions have undermined our perspective.

One of the pernicious side-effects of this is our inability and, in fact, our blind refusal to speak to the people who have and spend most of the money in our economy. As a recent research paper from the UK said about our industry...

"...we, like everyone else, prefer to talk to people we are familiar with and understand. Witness the industry's continued fixation with targeting 18-34... which is surely driven more by the composition of our industry than the demographic reality of our aging population and the massive concentration of wealth and spending"

The auto industry, which is the largest category of advertised goods, provides an excellent example. While car makers often feature young adults in their ads, adults under 25 comprise fewer than 1% of new car buyers. In the past 5 years, car ownership among 18-34 year olds has dropped 30%. Meanwhile, about 75% of new car buyers are over 40.

There are two reasons advertising agencies default to youth imagery. First, the people in agencies are overwhelmingly young and don't have the cultural vocabulary to speak comfortably to mature people. Look in any coffee shop and try to find someone in his 20's talking to someone in her 50's. I mean, other than saying, "Can I take your order?" When the people writing the ads are disconnected from the people buying the products, there is a problem. And while only six percent of agency employees are over fifty, fifty-seven percent of new car buyers are over fifty.

Second, binding to youth culture is such an easy and attractive way to seem relevant. Particularly if you have been seduced by advertising's feedback loop and don't understand the limited role young people actually play in our economy.

There is a lazy, unimaginative way to do advertising, and a difficult, inspired way. The lazy way has been the same for decades – find a pop song or celebrity and borrow some glow. The difficult, inspired way is to untether yourself from the banality of trendiness and search for something interesting to say.

Marketing by Selfie-Stick

According to Nielsen, people over 50 are the most valuable generation in the history of marketing. So why do we ignore them?

In order to understand this phenomenon, I think we need to talk about the make-up of the ad industry. Walk into any ad agency in the world and in 10 seconds something will become obvious. Everyone is young. While people over 50 comprise 47% of adults in the US, they comprise 6% of agency employees.

The reason we are always given for this is that young people are just more creative. Or as the insufferable Mark Zuckerberg says, *"Young people are just smarter."*

I would like to challenge this notion. To do so, I would like to go outside the advertising industry — which flatters itself with the idea of creativity — to other fields where creativity is absolutely essential. Let's look at the year 2017.

We'll start with the Nobel Prize. There is only one Nobel Prize in a creative field. It is the prize for Literature. It went to Kazuo Ishiguro who is 64.

The Pulitzer Prize is awarded in several creative fields. The Pulitzer for Drama went to Lynn Nottage who is 54. The Pulitzer for History went to Heather Ann Thompson, age 55. The Pulitzer for Poetry went to Tyehimba Jess, age 53.

Meanwhile at the Academy Awards, three of the four winners for acting were over 50: Francis McDormand, 60; Gary Oldman, 59, and Allison Janney, 58. The fourth, young Sam Rockwell, turned 50 the following month. The Oscar for Best Director went to Guillermo del Toro, who was 53.

Next we move to television. The Emmy for Best Drama Series went to The Handmaid's Tale. The novel was written by Margaret Atwood who was 79 and was creative consultant on the show. The Best Comedy Series went to Veep, executive produced by Julia Louis-Dreyfus, 57. She also won for Best Actress. Best Limited Series went to Big Little Lies created by David E Kelley, 62. The Best Supporting Actress was Ann Dowd, 62. Best Supporting Actor was John Lithgow, 73. Best Supporting Actor in a Comedy Series went to Alec Baldwin, 60.

So, let's recap. People over 50 are creative enough to dominate in Nobels, Pulitzers, Oscars, and Emmys but are *not* creative enough to write a fucking banner ad. I guarantee you, not one of these brilliantly talented people could get a job in an ad agency today. Not one.

Next, let's look at the facts about older consumers:
- In the U.S. people over 50 are responsible for over half of all consumer spending.
- They outspend the average consumer in nearly every category – food, household furnishings, entertainment, personal care, automotive...
- They account for 55% of all consumer packaged goods sales and dominate 94% of CPG categories
- They outspend other adults online 2:1 on a per-capita basis

- They have a net worth about three times that of other generations
- They buy about fifty-seven percent of all new cars.
- They control about seventy percent of wealth in the US
- If they were their own country, Americans over fifty would be the third largest economy in the world — bigger than the entire economies of Germany, Japan, or India.
- And the future? Between now and 2030 the population of adults over fifty will grow at about three times the rate of adults under fifty.

Do you really think it's a good idea to ignore these people? And yet, according to a 2016 study by Nielsen, people over 50 are the target for between five and ten percent of marketing activity in the US. While everyone in marketing is obsessed with millennials, we are actually going through one of the greatest demographic changes in human history and it is being completely ignored

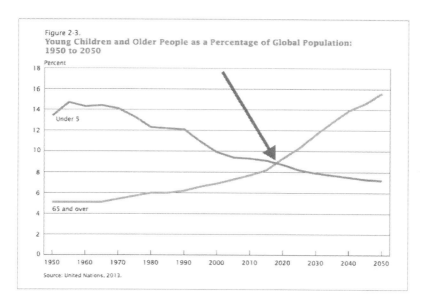

Figure 2-3.
Young Children and Older People as a Percentage of Global Population: 1950 to 2050

Source: United Nations, 2013.

This chart from the UN demonstrates an astounding demographic change that is occurring in just 100 years. In the year 1950, there were three times as many people in the world under 5 as there were over 65. By 2050 there will be twice as many people over 65 as there will be under 5. Our population is aging at a remarkable rate. But we in the ad and marketing business have invented all kinds of convenient bullshit for why we ignore mature people.

The real reason we ignore older people is...we hate them. We hate older people. Advertising people are young and they like the excitement of youth, not the boredom of middle age, or the frailties of old age. We can't build ourselves a hot advertising career by talking to old farts. Consequently, we have invented all kinds of bullshit to justify our malpractice. The neglect of mature consumers and pandering to young people is nothing but narcissism disguised as strategy. It is marketing by selfie-stick.

If we dropped ad people in from Mars and they looked at the data, they would understand in 60 seconds how important it is to aim marketing activity at people over 50. Unfortunately, our advertising leaders don't come from Mars. They come from marketingland where decades of prejudices and stupidity have overwhelmed simple, clear thinking.

PART FIVE: RECESS

Okay, you've made it this far, you deserve a break. Let's take a pause here for some sidelights and silliness and then we'll get back to the difficult work of calling everyone stupid.

Life in Conferenceland

One of the downsides of making your living as a loudmouth is that you have to do it in public. This means participating in conferences. As everyone knows, there's nothing in the world as dreary as a marketing conference, with the possible exception of a search engine optimization webinar or lunch with a CMO.

It is my good fortune that when I speak at conferences I am usually billed as the keynote, which often means I get to speak first. Speaking first has one great advantage. After I speak I can wait until no one's looking then sneak out the back door and find a nice quiet bar.

I was at a conference a few months ago and I decided to be mature and hang around and listen to some other speakers. I'll never make that mistake again. Here's what I learned:

- The future is going to be amazing. No one's going to have to do anything. Everything will be done for us by AI, or robots, or Jeff Bezos. We won't have to work, rotate our tires, or chew our food.

- Robots, by the way, will be stealing our jobs, our airline miles, and our children.

- Women will also be amazing. When they run everything there will be no poverty or inequality or wait times at the Genius Bar. Except for that crazy one from Theranos.

- Advertising, on the other hand, is not amazing. In fact, it's dead. It's going to be replaced by virtual reality or self-driving scooters or 5G or something.

- Better expect the unexpected because if you expect the expected than your expectations will be unexpectedly...I don't know...something very scary.

- China and India are going to have their own internets which will be better than ours because your password will be embedded in your brain or your kidneys and you won't have to update Flash every half hour.

- Data is not only the secret to marketing success, it also makes your car's engine run smoother and – something you probably didn't know – it makes a great Father's Day gift!

- Facebook is changing. No, really, they mean it this time! They're going to be double-extra careful with our data, our bank account numbers, and our drug bust records by taking all our files and putting them in Ziploc bags. And if anyone tries to break into them they will suspend them and not let them open another Facebook account for almost twenty minutes. Unless they use another name.

- Consumers love your brand and want a relationship with it and want to join the conversation about it and share it with their tribe... or, wait a minute... (DISSOLVE TO 30

MINUTES LATER)... brands mean nothing to consumers. The internet has disintermediated everything and the whole idea of brands is totally stupid and obsolete... (CUT TO PANEL DISCUSSION)

- Gen Z is a whole new species of human that is even cooler than millennials. You have to get rid of all those idiot millennials because they are stupid dinosaurs. If you don't have a Gen Z strategy in place by tomorrow 9 am you are already too late and you are dead. By the way, we are holding a 3-day Gen Z Insider Summit in Orlando next month...

- Consumers will love your brand of peanut milk *even more* if your brand purpose aligns with their values and they know you are committed to world peace and single-payer pet burials.

- And, by the way, everything is changing and if your business doesn't transform you will be left behind and die. It doesn't matter what you are, you have to transform into something else. It doesn't matter what you transform into as long as you stop doing whatever it is you are doing and start doing something that requires AI, robots, or Jeff Bezos.

Bottom line: The only sensible reason for attending a marketing conference is to get as far away as possible from the dreary *reality* of marketing. Like Disneyland, marketing's Conferenceland is much cleaner, prettier, and safer than the actual thing.

My advice is stay the hell away from marketing conferences unless, of course, I'm speaking. In which case, bring the whole family.

My B2B Dream

I had a dream about B2B advertising last night. I heard somebody say...

We want to become your customer experience partner. We'll help you architect cutting-edge systems, both human and virtual, from high-quality product provision to unique problem resolution through customized resource management solutions.

We are laser-focused on re-imagining customer experience and future-proofing your business. In doing so, we also provide hands-on training to keep your employees engaged, more productive, and up to date on all aspects of your integrated solution stack.

Regardless of what industry you're in, we have the answers for your resource and system needs. Our data-driven, turn-key deliverables protect your most valuable assets - your customer relationships! We have the ability to work with many different industries, quickly responding to changing applications and environments, while staying focused on quality and best-in-class performance.

We analyze your historical and forecasted needs to ensure high execution while reducing costs.

Our experienced experts will visit your distributed work environments and evaluate your operating modalities to advise on enhancements that will improve your key measurables and create ongoing alignment with sales and engagement goals. They'll deliver detailed reports and recommend solutions tailored to your toughest KPI challenges.

Here are some ways that our eBusiness solutions can benefit you:

- *Dynamic integration*
- *Catalog extracts*
- *Process regeneration*

We are committed to both innovation and speedy adoption of disruptive sales-side ecosystems.

Our highly-trained associates take your operating blueprint and provide you with a finished global solution. The final resource set will be of the highest quality and will be validated and delivered with robust support structures. Additionally, we will source and integrate these structures into your assembly per your stated requirements.

In short, we are inverting the traditional systems architecture stack and abandoning outmoded team structures in favor of high-octane solutions that supercharge opportunities for growth.

We want to be your total resource solutions partner!

I awakened with a jolt, sat up and screamed, "Okay. But what the fuck do you *DO*?"

Everything I Know about Advertising
I Learned From a Blues Song

I was wasting time on the web the other day and I came upon an article called *"Let's Talk About How to Build a Brand."* There was nothing terribly wrong with the piece if you're the kind of person who likes to read instruction manuals. It was kind of the 30-minute version of Marketing 101. But, like so much of marketing thinking today, it was all brains and no guts.

It reminded me of my *Aha!* advertising moment when I realized how the whole thing works – when I realized that it's not about how *marketing* works, it's about how *people* work.

I was listening to an album by Ry Cooder called *Paradise and Lunch*, a monstrously great album. One of the tunes on the album is called *Feelin' Good*, which was written by a blues singer named J.B. Lenoir.

In two lines, Lenoir made me realize how simple the whole thing is and how stupid I'd been not to understand what was right in front of me. He tells us more about how marketing works than all the books in the worldwide marketing library...

"Feelin' good, feelin' good
All the money in the world spent on feelin' good"

And after years of toiling in advertising I finally understood how this thing works. People buy what they believe will make them feel good.

Why do they buy an iPhone instead of a Samsung? Because they believe it will make them feel better. A Ford instead of a Chevy? Because they believe it will make them feel good. A Bud versus a Coors? Because they believe it will make them feel good.

They don't buy things to be part of a tribe, or to have a brand relationship, or to do any of the prodigiously analytical things our marketing prophets tell us. What our experts are seeing is what it looks like from the outside.

What people are actually doing is buying what they believe will make them feel good.

Next time you sit down to create or evaluate an ad, remember this…
"All the money in the world spent on feelin' good."

Death at Cannes

For the 100th consecutive year I did not go to Cannes. But the good thing is, I know exactly what happened and saved myself thousands of dollars. As a free service to you other losers who didn't attend, here's what you missed

- A very casually dressed ceo from a very big holding company said that the consumer is changing and we have to change to keep up with the changing consumer. He said we have to evolve or die.

- A very rich and famous creative person gave a very stirring speech about how creativity is the heart and soul of our industry and we have to get back to celebrating creativity. Agencies that don't prioritize creativity will soon be dead.

- Another famous creative person with very expensive eye-wear said we need to be brave. Those that aren't brave won't live long.

- A very earnest female executive gave a talk about how we have to value all people regardless of sex, gender orientation, race, religion, absence of religion, age, ability, body type or gluten sensitivity. Marketers that don't value diversity will soon be extinct.

- A very European planner gave a talk about how we have to stop thinking short-term and realize that brands are built by long-term strategy. Those who focus on the short-term will disappear in the long-term. (Then she hurried out to see how many tweets her talk got.)

- A panel discussion was held to discuss the future of marketing. It was agreed that more personalization was necessary to make marketing more relevant to consumers. Brands that don't have better insights into individual consumer behavior don't have long to live.

- A panel discussion was held to discuss the future of the agency business. It was agreed that the agency business must align its priorities to the evolving needs of our clients or we will fade away.

- A very famous celebrity from outside the advertising industry gave a talk on why he/she now pays as much attention to social media as he/she does to acting/singing/basketball. *"You have to stay in touch to stay alive."*

- A very famous billionaire sent a very mid-level executive to explain how their company is committed to protecting consumer privacy by developing an AI process to screen out everything and everyone that is bad. *"If we don't do that, we have no future."*

- A research expert said that in order to understand Gen Z we must forget everything we know about millennials, who were digital natives, and start to understand Gen Z, who are "digital aboriginals." Ignoring the needs of Gen Z is a death sentence.

- A panel of branding experts agreed that consumers now expect brands to be socially responsible and make the world a better place for all people regardless of sex, gender orientation, race, religion, absence of religion, age, ability, body type or gluten sensitivity. Brands that don't do that will soon die out.

There is so much potential for death in the advertising business these days that there is only one responsible way to avoid marketing's grim reaper – go to Cannes, hang out on yachts and gulp putrid rosé.

Thank goodness there are thousands of men and women from around the world who are willing to do this on our behalf. Otherwise, we'd be dead.

PART SIX: DANGER

The ad industry has evolved from silly to dangerous

The Fraud Factory

"I have studied the economic costs of fraud in many sectors for decades, and I was left stunned by the scale of fraud in online advertising," says Professor Roberto Cavazo of the University of Baltimore.

One of the great promises of online advertising was that it would lead to more accountability because it would be more measurable. It has turned out to be more measurable, but the problem is we don't know what the hell we're measuring. The unreliability of the metrics we get,, and the torrent of fraud are so massive that accountability is more faith than fact.

By most measures only about 50% of traffic on the web is *human*. The rest are bots, scrapers, hackers, spammers and other impersonators. Not all bots are bad, nonetheless, the amount of fraud being perpetrated on advertisers by online scammers is astounding.

Professor Cavazo participated in a study conducted by cybersecurity firm Cheq called *'The Economic Cost of Bad Actors on the Internet, Ad Fraud 2019."* According to The Drum, the report states that the *"Cost of Global Ad Fraud Could Top $30bn"* this year.

This report is one of many that repudiate the recent nonsense promulgated by the ANA (Association of National Advertisers) which claimed that the *"War On Ad Fraud Is Succeeding"* and that fraud would fall to about $5 billion in 2019 from $7.2 billion last year.

According to The Drum, *"...studies, which pin the cost of ad fraud at about $7.2bn per year, fail to capture the full extent of the damage...These studies often extrapolate from limited samples...Such studies also restrict the scope of their research to botnets, which are just one source of ad fraud..."*

The feckless ANA and other advertising trade associations continue to cover their asses and mislead their members, the industry, and the public about the extent of criminal activity that is polluting online advertising and costing advertisers tens of billions.

The digital advertising director of the *Financial Times*, Anthony Hitchings, who also participated in the study mentioned above had this to say, *"The scale of the fraud we found is jaw-dropping. The industry continues to waste marketing budgets on what is essentially organized crime."*

In 2018, the same year the ANA said fraud had dropped by 10%, *JPMorgan Chase* reported that ad fraud had grown by over 100%. That year, Jupiter research estimated online ad fraud at $19 billion.

In a report by Adobe, quoted in *The Wall Street Journal*...

"...about 28% of website traffic showed strong "non-human signals," leading the company to believe that the traffic came from bots or click farms."

Using Adobe's 28% number and projecting this out over $237 billion in estimated online ad spending in 2019, online ad fraud could easily have reached tens of billions.

Kevin Frisch, the former head of performance marketing and CRM at Uber, tells the story of how ad fraud (specifically attribution fraud) was headed toward eating $120 million of Uber's $150 million online ad budget. *"We turned off 2/3 of our spend, we turned off 100 million of annual spend out of 150, and basically saw no change..."*

Dr. Augustine Fou, PhD from MIT who has taught at NYU and who is one of the leading experts on ad fraud, estimates that online ad fraud stole over $58 billion of the $106 billion spent on online advertising in the US in 2018. That's over 50% of online ad dollars.

In 2017, a fraud called Fireball was discovered. It had infected 250 million computers and 20% of corporate computer networks worldwide. According to Dr. Fou, this operation was capable of producing 30 billion fraudulent ad impressions a minute. If you told me it could produce 30 billion a *year*, I'd be shocked. But 30 billion a minute? Dr. Fou called this "*...fraud on such a massive scale it is beyond belief.*"

The truth is nobody knows the exact extent of ad fraud. The whole art and science of fraud is to avoid detection. The only ad frauds we know about are the ones we've been able to detect. In other words, the ones that aren't very good. But there is no doubt about one thing — ad fraud is enormous. According to the World Federation of Advertisers, by 2025 ad fraud may be the second largest source of criminal revenue *in the world*, after drug trafficking.

Fraud is found in every aspect of online commerce, not just advertising. A startling example is provided by *The Washington Post*. They say that in a twelve month period spanning the end of 2017 and the beginning of 2018, Facebook had to remove 2.8 billion fake accounts from its platform. That means they removed almost three times as many fake accounts as there are human beings in the Western Hemisphere.

But it's not just fraud, fake accounts, and viewability problems that are wasting advertisers' dollars online. According to The Guardian, and confirmed by the WFA, between 40 and 70 percent of online advertising dollars are scraped by adtech middlemen.

The path a typical programmatically bought online ad takes from advertiser to publisher weaves its way through trading desks, DSPs (Demand Side Platforms), data providers, targeting programs, verification software, SSPs (Supply Side Platforms,) ad exchanges — an insane and murky gauntlet of toll takers who each extract a little money from the advertiser's media budget. Each also provides an opportunity for crooks to squeeze some cash from the process.

The ANA says that of every dollar an online advertiser spends, only 25 cents reaches the consumer. The rest is extracted by fees, commissions and bad actors. And if Lumen, a British research company is correct, only 9% of online ads are ever even noticed for a second. You can calculate 9% of 25 cents for yourself to see how much of your ad dollar even *has a chance* to influence someone.

Perhaps the most damning aspect of digital advertising measurement is that the more you know about the subject the more you understand how corrupt and unreliable it is.

Aram Zucker-Scharff, adtech director at *The Washington Post* says, *"The numbers are all f**king fake, the metrics are bullshit, the* *agencies responsible for enforcing good practices are knowing bullshitters enforcing and profiting off all the fake numbers..."*

Ellen Pao, former CEO of Reddit says, *"It's all true. Everything is fake."*

Conspiracy of Silence

For several years the advertising industry has been engaged in a conspiracy to deceive its clients and the public about online advertising.

It is not the kind of conspiracy you get when bad people get together to plot a crime. It is the kind of conspiracy you get when frightened people individually decide it is wiser to keep their mouths shut than question the status quo.

For the last few years we have been flooded with scandals and revelations about corruption, fraud, and lies in the online advertising ecosystem. Here is just a partial list in no particular order:

- Tens of billions of dollars in online ad fraud

- Inflated and absurd "metrics" from Facebook

- Advertising dollars going to support terrorist, nazi, and pornography sites

- Advertisers unknowingly supporting pedophile rings on YouTube

- Billion dollar fraud in influencer followers

- Traffic fraud

- Criminal federal investigation of Facebook data sharing

- The UK's Information Commissioner's Office stating that adtech is "illegal" and "out of   control"

- A report from the Association of National Advertisers claiming that corruption and kickbacks were "pervasive" in the advertising industry.

- Massive fraud in social media followers.

- Click farms going 24-hours a day.

- Numerous scandals involving online publishers, search engines, and browsers spying on people without their knowledge or consent.

- Sharing of "secure" personal information among web entities.

- FBI and Justice Department investigations of media practices.

The terribly damning part of all this is that there are only two possibilities: Either agencies are remarkably stupid and don't know what is going on, or they know and are keeping their mouths shut. It's hard to decide which is worse.

I believe they have been engaged in an unspoken conspiracy.

Not a single one of the scandals listed above were brought to light by a media agency. Not one. Let's put this another way – not one of the scandals about online media were exposed by the people *whose job it is to scrutinize online media.*

Agencies, particularly media agencies, are as close to the online media industry as you can get. They are analyzing online media 24 hours a day. They are responsible for seeing to it that hundreds of billions of online advertising dollars are spent properly every year. They work very closely with media. They have the facts at their fingertips. They are assessing online media opportunities on behalf of their clients every minute of every day.

How can it be that reporters, who are not trained in media, have not nearly the resources to scrutinize media, and have no expertise in analyzing media, were able to sniff out scandal after scandal while the "experts" were not able to do so? It is not possible. It doesn't even pass the giggle test. As one very highly regarded media analyst commented to me recently, *"agency bigwigs are notoriously paranoid and fearful. There's a strong code of silence..."*

If it were left to the leaders of the ad industry, we would know nothing about any of the appalling stories listed above. By concealing their knowledge of deceit and dishonesty in online media, and by Fear Of Finding Out (FOFO) the ad industry has failed at one of their most consequential responsibilities - being trustworthy stewards of their clients' money. Instead, they have been responsible for wasting billions of client dollars. Why?

- Because they're afraid to admit they've been played for fools by online media.
- Because they get fees or commissions on much of the wasted billions.

Is it any wonder marketers are moving media functions in-house? One can only wonder what additional sleaze the media "experts" are keeping quiet about.

The ad industry has allowed itself to crawl into bed with the weasels at Facebook, Google and the rest of the devious adtech squids. It makes us look like fools. Every week there are alarming reports of fraud, corruption, privacy abuse, and security failures in online media and we shrug our shoulders and duck for cover.

The ad industry, controlled by misguided and incompetent leadership at trade associations and holding companies, had better get its act together. By being lapdogs to the corrupt and dangerous online media we are quickly squandering what's left of our credibility.

We are on the wrong side of history and will continue to stay there until the silent conspiracy to protect online media ends.

Totalitarian Marketing

A few years ago I wrote a book called *BadMen* about the dangers of tracking and online surveillance. Consequently I am not going to take a lot of time in this book to explore the issue. Instead I'm going to do a brief summary of the dangers inherent.

Advertising used to be concerned with imparting information. Today it is equally concerned with collecting information. To a substantial degree, what we call online advertising isn't really advertising at all. It is spyware whose greatest value may not be in delivering information to us, but in collecting information about us. As Doc Searls says, online advertising is "tracking-aimed junk mail that only looks like ads."

Online advertising is largely reliant on "tracking" to accomplish its goals. Tracking is just a pleasanter word for surveillance. Our web browsers, our search engines, and the sites we visit use invisible software to keep track of everything we do and everywhere we go online and in the physical world. Our emails and texts are read or scanned and archived by the providers we use. Our physical movements are tracked, recorded, and sold to marketers and black marketeers. The data that is harvested about us is re-sold to "data brokers" who then re-resell to anyone with a dollar. All this information is floating around without our knowledge or consent. It has proven to be easily accessible to hackers, foreign governments, and other malefactors.

Google, Facebook, Amazon and other online media properties have created amazing stuff. The products they have created, the services they provide, and the technology they have given us are unprecedented and sometimes wonderful and brilliant. But in the process they have also created an unnecessarily monstrous, mostly invisible, highly dangerous hidden world of information collection and distribution about us that is also unprecedented — and fraught with peril.

According to The Wall Street Journal, Facebook's most recent user agreement contains the following:

- Facebook maintains the right to collect your phone number and other information about you when anyone, including people you don't know, upload their contacts that may include you.

- Even when you turn off location services, Facebook tracks your location through Wi-Fi access points, cell towers and IP addresses.

- You probably think Facebook is collecting data about you from the device you're using. Silly you. If you are anywhere near any other devices on your network they are collecting info from those devices as well. It's magic!

- Facebook tracks you through third parties whether or not you are logged into Facebook.

- And the pièce de résistance – Facebook's new data policy asserts that they track you even if you don't have a Facebook account.

The preposterous rationale for all this abuse of our privacy is that it helps marketers provide us with "more relevant advertising." As if the citizens of the world are taking to the streets demanding more relevant advertising.

We were taught to fear totalitarian governments. We feared they would know everything about us, follow us everywhere, know who we were talking to and what we were saying, and keep secret files about us which could be used to influence our lives in ways that were only vaguely visible to us.

We are well on our way to such a nightmare. Except it isn't necessarily our government that knows everything about us, follows us everywhere, knows who we are talking to and what we are saying, and keeps secret files about us. It is the marketing industry.

We know where totalitarian government leads. It lead to Iron Curtains, Gestapos, and KGBs. It leads to the trivialization of personal freedoms and the unchecked power of tyrants. We don't know where totalitarian *marketing* leads. There is no precedent for it. But it's hard to come up with a scenario that leads to anything good.

Surveillance marketing is little more than ten years old but has already played a significant role in undermining our confidence in the legitimacy of our elections and the credibility of our news media. Tracking is a danger to democratic societies and to individual citizens.

The online advertising and media industries claim that this type of spying is necessary for their business model. It's nonsense. Traditional media - TV, radio, print, outdoor - did very well, thank you, for years without surveillance. There is no reason online advertising can't be viable without spying on us.

Marketers claim that precise data collection is essential to their survival because it helps them find the most likely customers for their products and provide those customers with relevant information. Let's pretend for a minute that this bullshit is true. So what? Since when did the convenience of marketers become more important than the privacy rights of citizens?

The Good in Online Advertising

Online advertising has been so debased by creeps and crooks, and oversold by hustlers and liars, that it is sometimes difficult for us to appreciate the good in it. If we could eliminate the creeps, crooks and hustlers, and allow the web to provide what it is capable of providing...well, that's what this essay is about.

The best part of online advertising is that it funds an amazing array of free stuff

A look at the numbers illustrates clearly how much we value what we get online. The average person in America now spends almost four hours a day online. This is not inconsiderable. And we wouldn't be there if we weren't getting value from it.

The key piece is this: Virtually everything we enjoy about the web is paid for by advertising. Whether you hate advertising or love it, there is one simple truth that must be acknowledged – advertising provides the money for companies to create the stuff we like and use online. This is why it is important to preserve an ad-supported web.

There is nothing intrinsically wrong with online advertising. But there is something terribly wrong with the flavor of online advertising that we have evolved.

Essentially there are two kinds of online advertising. The good kind supports quality publishers, does not spy on us or track our every move, and respects our privacy by not collecting unnecessary personal, private information. It doesn't share it, sell it, or leak it into the digi-sphere.

The bad kind of online advertising is only superficially advertising. It is mostly tracking-based spyware disguised as advertising distributed primarily by machines ("programmatically.")

The bad kind is the kind that the online media industry has defaulted to. It supports the shittiest publishers by using software to find the cheapest, crappiest environments to distribute ads to, thereby stealing money from quality publishers and giving birth to self-inflicted brand safety issues.

Because its primary model is data-based direct marketing (what we used to call "junk mail") it leads to a style of "click here" advertising that magnifies the most annoying and intrusive aspects of advertising.

The politics of online advertising is the part that I find most bewildering. For over a decade, the powerful players in the advertising world have been working relentlessly against their own interests.

Advertisers would be much better served if they knew where their ads were running; if their budgets were spent on working media rather than wasted on adtech middlemen; if their ads were appearing on high quality sites instead being "programmatically" strewn all over trash sites; if tens of billions of dollars weren't being stolen by criminals with fraudulent websites and imaginary viewers; if hundreds of millions of people were not blocking ads.

All of these problems could be significantly reduced by doing one simple thing – ending tracking. And yet the moment there is a suggestion of setting some limitations on the ability of online advertisers, media, and publishers to spy on us, the advertisers rise up through their tainted trade organizations to oppose it.

The same is true of publishers. Quality online publishers are having their audiences and revenue stolen from them through data leakage (in which programmatic systems follow valuable customers to cheaper sites and reach them there.) They are victims of criminal activities like fraudulent lookalike websites stealing their audiences and ad revenues. They are losing more than half their potential revenue to the sinkhole of adtech middlemen. They have lost control of their brand identities by allowing automated systems to determine who and what can be advertised on their sites. And they are losing revenue as ad blocking continues unabated.

And yet, once again, the moment the subject of limiting the slimy hands of tracking and adtech come up, they mostly oppose what is clearly in their own best interest.

Online advertising doesn't have to be...

  - despised by the public

  - a subversive force to democratic institutions

  - corrupt and fraud ridden

  - a medium for criminals to find valuable personal and private information about us

  - a source of harm to legitimate online publishers

  - a multi-billion dollar source of fraud for advertisers

  - a degrading factor in news media and journalism

Online advertising supports so many good things that we enjoy and appreciate about the web. It gives us entertainment and information. It allows us to befriend people we would otherwise never know.

It would take so little for the online ad industry to do so much good – for itself and for the public. Ending tracking is not a panacea to all the problems of the digital world. But it is a great place to start.

We have decades of evidence that tracking is not a necessity for advertising success. TV never tracked us. Radio never tracked us. Newspapers and magazines never tracked us. And we have more than enough evidence that adtech is in many ways not just non-productive, but counterproductive.

We need to get rid of tracking – not advertising – to make the web what it ought to be.

PART SEVEN: ADVICE

I met a guy the other day who didn't have a podcast

Caution

We've reached the point in the book at which the author offers his recipe for how to cure all the ills of the world. In other words, the bullshit part of the book.

Just like the history of advertising, the future is built on likelihoods, probabilities, randomness, and luck. The likelihood of my ideas being anything other than wishful thinking are extremely low. The probability of anyone taking my suggestions seriously hovers very close to zero.

Consequently, instead of offering you a bunch of mile-wide solutions that the industry is certain to ignore, I'm going to suggest some personal suggestions that you can use for thinking about what you're doing.

What follows are a few ideas that I hope will allow you to approach the subject of advertising with an intelligent dose of reality and a healthy degree of skepticism (or if you're a Brit, scepticism.)

Advertising Is a Weak Force

Gravity is everywhere. Consequently, we think of gravity as a powerful force that keeps us glued to the ground and brings down huge airplanes. Actually, science tells us that gravity is a very weak force. In fact, it is the weakest force in the universe.

To prove this to yourself, go to a children's toy shop and buy one of those little 50-cent horseshoe magnets. Then put a paper clip on the ground. Place the magnet near the paper clip. You now have two competing forces – the electro-magnetic force of the kids' magnet versus the gravitational force of the entire planet.

The magnet wins. The electro-magnetic force is actually 1,000,000,000,000,000,000,000,000,000,000,000,000 times stronger than gravity. But because gravity is all around us, we think of it as a strong force.

The same is true of advertising. We are exposed to thousands of advertising messages every day. Only a tiny proportion of them have any impact on us at all. As a whole, advertising is a weak force. But like the airplane falling to earth, every now and then there is a big advertising event and the ad industry takes it as proof of the extraordinary power of ads. In fact, it is proof of only one thing — the extraordinary power of *great* ads.

In fact, there are only two ways in which big advertising successes usually occur — great creative work or large expenditures of money.

One way to be successful at advertising is to spend a lot of money. Think about McDonald's, and Toyota, and Pepsi, and Coors. None of them has done a memorable ad in years. And yet they remain at the top of their categories in part due to the force of their spending. If you are planning for great success through advertising, you better be ready to commit yourself to either doing great creative work or spending a lot.

Obviously, doing outstanding creative work is a far more desirable strategy. The problem is that doing great ads is way more difficult than it sounds. You've probably noticed that about 95% of all ads are crappy and derivative. And so are about the same percent of books, songs, and paintings.

If you think all this crappy stuff is around because people aren't trying very hard, you're wrong. The reason is actually quite simple: producing great stuff is really, really hard. And there are very few people who can do it. Nobody sets out to create a crappy TV spot or a crappy book or a crappy song. They just turn out that way.

Creative talent is a very rare and very precious commodity. Not everyone has it. As a matter of fact, hardly anyone has it. That's why our industry's obsession with data and metrics has been so damaging. We've forgotten what got us here.

Nobody Gives a Flying Shit about Your Brand.

Okay, I'm overstating the case a little here, but it's still a good policy to live by.

Yes, there are a few "Ms. Popularity" brands that people care about. And yes, we each have a handful of brands we are attached to. But for the most part, Mr. Marketer, nobody cares deeply about your pickles, your half-and-half, your mayonnaise, your cookies, your tires, chewing gum, toothbrush, umbrella, dishwasher, napkins, toaster, gasoline, horseradish, dental floss, paper towels, golf balls, shoe laces, pillows, pencils, deodorant, nail clippers, furniture polish, frozen chicken strips, lamps, potting soil, bathing caps, glassware, clocks, fungicide, dish towels, cat litter, sun block, cookie dough, motor oil, light bulbs, burglar alarm, ironing board, fire insurance, coffee filters, pillow cases, mouthwash, vacuum cleaner bags, shower curtains, and the thousand other things they buy every year.

If you believe that people are online every day having "brand conversations" about any of this crap you're an idiot. Branding experts tell us that...

- Consumers want to "join the conversation" about brands, and co-create with brands
- Brands need to create a community of engaged consumers to be successful
- A brand that aligns with our values will be rewarded by consumers sharing their enthusiasm for the brand with their online community

Really? Let's have a look at *your* behavior and see how it correlates with the beliefs of these experts.

Think about your refrigerator. Think about all the stuff that's in there: The cheese, the juices, the jelly, the butter, the beer, the soda, the mayonnaise, the bacon, the mustard...

Now think about your pantry. The cereals, the beans, the napkins, the flour, the detergent, the sugar, the rice, the bleach, the paper towels...

Next your medicine cabinet. The toothpaste, the pain relievers, the shampoo, the soap, the band-aids, the deodorant, the cosmetics...

Now your closet and dresser. Your socks, your underwear, your shirts, your pajamas, your swim suit, your t-shirts, your sweaters, your jeans, your sneakers...

Now your garage. The battery, the tires, the wiper blades, motor oil, gasoline, the air filter, the muffler...

Now answer these questions:

- Do you "share branded content" about any of this stuff?

- Do you feel "personally engaged" with these brands?

- Do you "join the conversation" about any of this stuff?

- Do you ever "co-create" with any of these brands?

- Do you feel like you are part of these brand's "tribes" or "communities?"

Now answer this: If you don't, why in the freaking world do you believe anyone else does?

In fact, a smart marketer assumes that no one gives a flying shit about her brand. She assumes that she has to prove its value to her customers every day of the year. She takes nothing for granted. She does not believe that there are hoards of "brand ambassadors" out there in cyberland "advocating" for her brand. If there are some, great. But she's not going to count on it.

For a smart marketer, every day is Groundhog Day. Every day you have to get up, drag your ass to work, and remind the world – once again – why they should buy your stuff.

That's why god created advertising.

The Best Ad Strategy Is a Good Idea

Take those words and print them in letters a mile high and paste them over your desk. Oh, I forgot, nobody has a desk anymore...put them under your table or something.

Most of what goes on in ad agencies and marketing departments is a sham. It's useless meetings about worthless memos and useless memos about worthless meetings. I'm sorry to have to say it, but I suspect you probably know it's true.

Despite our obsessions with data and planning and strategy and all the other busywork that keeps us occupied all day, the best advertising strategy is a good idea. A large part of what we call "advertising strategy" is mostly window-dressing that is lost on consumers. Sure, every now and then someone comes up with a unique ad strategy but most of the brilliant ad strategies that appear in the lore of advertising weren't brilliant strategies at all. They were great creative ideas that were reverse engineered to appear to have been the result of brilliant strategy.

Most of the advertising we all remember is remembered because of a wonderful idea. If you don't believe this you don't belong in advertising. Become a brand manager or something.

Beware the Tyranny of Strategy

Strategies are not written by God. They are written by planners, researchers, account execs, clients and other mildly deranged mortals. Good creative people sometimes have a better feel for the problem than the committee that wrote the strategy. Sadly, they are often confronted with the brief only after the Committee of the Deranged have committed it to the inflexible logic of official documents..

When you are evaluating a campaign idea that does not conform to the brief, it's not enough to say 'this is off strategy'. You must also ask yourself, 'is this a better strategy than the one the committee came up with?'

If the answer is yes, you're going to have a lousy week. You have to go back and unsell a strategy that has probably taken months to develop, has been up and down the client organization, and has lots of (probably questionable) data to back it up. Somehow, you have to convince a whole bunch of people that the work they've been doing for the past few months is wrong.

Sound impossible? That's why you get the big bucks.

Be Eternally Skeptical of Grand Strategic Insights

Planners, researchers and their ilk love to take a little information and turn it into a heroic vision. Beware of this. Most valuable insights are small and contingent. There is almost nothing you can say about human behavior that is universal. Including this.

I was once at an advertising conference and a planning director was making a presentation. She was talking about groups she was conducting for a bank. The groups were going nowhere. She asked a participant "If you could invent the perfect bank, what would it be like?" He sat there for a minute or two without answering.

"I suddenly realized," she said, "I had the answer right there before me. People don't want to think about their bank. Then I knew I had the strategy: "Bank of Whatever. It's the bank you don't have to think about."

I have a different explanation for the above. She asked an incredibly stupid question and the respondent sat there dazed and confused.

From the flimsiest of observations, she drew a grand, dumb conclusion. And worst of all, the agency and the client bought it.

In the world today, a thousand brands will change their strategy. Remember, in every case the strategy they are discarding was once the product of somebody's grand strategic insight.

Simplify and Specify

I've seen thousands of ads that were too complicated or too generic. I've never seen one that was too simple or too specific.

The Opposite of Data

You don't have to spend much time around marketers to realize that every few years the industry discovers a new miracle and becomes obsessed with it. Our latest marvel-du-jour is data.

You can tell it's an official miracle by the number of dreary conferences held to talk it to death, and the number of nitwits that can't finish a sentence without invoking its name. But I have a thought I'd like you to consider.

• Do you think Coke has data that Pepsi doesn't have?
• Do you think McDonald's has data that Burger King doesn't have?
• Do you think Ford has data that Chevy doesn't have?

Here's my point – just about the same data is available to just about everyone who wants it. And if you don't have it, with about two clicks of a mouse you can buy it.

It's not the data that makes the difference, it's what you do with it.

Give a mediocre person or company all the data in the world and they'll come up with garbage. Give a brilliant person or company one critical fact and they'll build you an industry.

Hundreds of physicists had the same data as Einstein. But Einstein had something they didn't – the creative brilliance to formulate a vision of what the data meant.

You don't need an MBA to figure out that many of the really huge marketing successes of the last century did not come from data analysis, business models, strategic exercises or professional marketers. They came from drop-outs or daydreamers with a hunch:

- Steve Jobs
- Walt Disney
- J.K. Rowling
- Bill Gates
- Mark Zuckerberg

I could go on...

The advertising industry – whose only important asset is ideas – has learned nothing from this. We keep heading in the wrong direction. We keep bulking up everything in our arsenal except our creative resources. Then we take the people who are supposed to be our idea people and give them till 3 o'clock to do a banner.

Sure, we need people who are tech-savvy and analytical. But more than anything, we need some brains-in-a-bottle who have no responsibility other than to sit in a corner and feed us crazy ideas. We keep looking to "transform" our industry but ignore the one transformation that would kill.

Just a cursory look at the output of most agencies and marketing companies will convince anyone that what we are producing is different versions of the same things.

I am not suggesting for a moment that the development of big ideas is easy or can be formularized. Nor am I suggesting that having information thwarts creativity. What I am suggesting is that creativity is being subsumed by our obsessions with other things.

Our industry is drowning in math and starving for ideas. We need people who can dream shit up. We need impractical, illogical people.

We have plenty of data. We need more of the opposite.

ACKNOWLEDGEMENTS

It takes a pillage... so I would like to thank and apologize to the people I stole ideas, insights, opinions, and terminology from to create this book. Some of you don't know that you unwittingly influenced my thinking. I'm afraid it's a burden you're going to have to live with: Byron Sharp, Mark Ritson, Dave Trott, Rory Sutherland, Rich Siegel, George Tannenbaum, Jay Tannenbaum, Jim Knapp, Sharon Krinsky, Claudia Caplan, Augustine Fou, Shailin Dhar, Praneet Sharma, Don Marti, Karen Nelson-Field, Richard Shotten, Peter Field, Les Binet, Tom Denford and probably some others who I can't think of at the moment.

I also want to thank Jean Robaire and Bonnie Miguel for their invaluable help in design and production. And finally, Maria Winston and Lucy Hoffman for allowing me to be a nuisance and torture them with doubt and questions.

ABOUT THE AUTHOR

Bob Hoffman lives in Oakland, California with his wife and dogs.

He has been CEO of three successful advertising agencies.

He retired from active duty in the agency business in 2013. To the dismay of many he has continued writing and speaking about it.

Printed in Great Britain
by Amazon